THE WORK OF THE MINISTER OF YOUTH, REVISED

Richard Ross, Compiler

Convention Press ● Nashville, Tennessee

CONTENTS

PREFACE

A child reared by his natural parents represents a synthesis of both the old and the new. His chromosomes carry genetic codes that tie him to his parents and other preceding generations. His developing personality has also been stamped with scores of environmental experiences with parents and other relatives.

At the same time a child represents something fresh. She is much more than the sum of the two sets of chromosomes she carries. She has a unique way of internalizing experiences. She is closely tied to her heritage, but she is also something new.

The same is true with *The Work of the Minister of Youth, Revised.* This fresh look at the role of the youth minister builds on a rich heritage. The original book, released in 1982, represented one of the first resources specifically targeted to Southern Baptist youth ministry professionals. It affirmed concepts of ministry that have become widespread in Southern Baptist life.

The original book carried the unmistakable mark of its compiler, Bob R. Taylor. Taylor, the first youth ministry consultant in the Church Administration Department at the Sunday School Board, guided the development of the first resources for Southern Baptist youth ministers. Taylor's writing and speaking made a lasting difference in the direction of Southern Baptist youth ministry.

This book builds on the strengths of its predecessor. The chapter on the youth minister's heritage contains new material on the history of adolescence and the roots of contemporary youth ministry. The chapter on the youth minister's philosophy presents for the first time the most common models of Southern Baptist youth ministry and the strengths and weaknesses of each.

The original book introduced the thought of ministry to three target groups: youth, parents of youth, and workers with youth. This revision expands on that concept by designating three full chapters to those target groups.

CHAPTER 1

THE MINISTER OF YOUTH'S HERITAGE

The contemporary minister of youth has a rich heritage. Those who understand the birth and development of this unique ministry position will be better able to chart a direction for the future.

The First Appearance of "Youth"

Today teenagers hold a special place in society. This has not always been true. These people generally were not viewed as somehow distinct from other ages until the rise of industrialization. Until that time, the human life cycle was viewed as having only two states, childhood and adulthood.

"Sociologists of education have discovered that in our own society, in the nineteenth century and in earlier times when most families sent out their children into the world of work at an early age, the break between childhood

Richard Ross
Youth ministry
consultant
Church
Administration
Department
Sunday School Board
Nashville, Tennessee

The chapter on administrative and planning skills presents techniques and procedures that frequently determine the effectiveness of ministry. The chapter on the youth minister's role with the denomination is all new. The chapter presents valuable help at every level of Southern Baptist life as well as practical contributions the youth minister can make to the denomination.

Authors Phil Briggs and Jerry Pounds are indicative of the quality of specific education most of our seminaries are providing for ministers of youth. Dennis Rogers, Chris Liebrum, J. B. Collingsworth, Dave Fuller, and Bill Falkner are indicative of the quality of leadership most states are providing for the minister of youth. Southern Baptists lead all other denominations in providing for youth ministers such competent and committed professors and leaders.

Judi Hayes is the editor of this resource. Her staff positions in local church youth ministry and her ongoing love for teenagers have equipped her to guide the development of the book. Judi's sharp intellect and vital interest in youth ministry have made a significant contribution to Southern Baptist life. Youth ministers are fortunate to have her on their team.

and adulthood was clearly marked and was not elongated by a period of transition. The same has been observed in nonindustrial societies, where children who come to their pubescence are passed quickly into adulthood through a very short tunnel, a ritual of transition or a rite of passage."[1]

The Industrial Revolution changed many facets of Western culture. One of those changes was a new way of viewing youth, making a more lengthy transition between childhood and adulthood. Adolescence and youth were "creations of a twentieth-century culture whose value on extended education and on growth and improvement of individuals has constructed a space of the life cycle for the express purpose of development, transition, change, struggle, improvement of self in the journey toward adulthood."[2]

Concerned Christians began to see these persons making the transition to adulthood as having unique needs, potential, and significance. Such a view marks a beginning of modern youth ministry.[3]

Early Youth Movements

"Sunday School, the Young Men's and Women's Christian Associations, and faith missionary societies were all significant movements of the nineteenth century." They quickly spread from England to America. Robert Raikes began a Sunday School in Glouchester, England, in 1780. The YWCA was organized in the 1840s, and the YMCA followed two decades later.[4]

The Student Volunteer Movement was a powerful force among college students from 1891 to 1910. Its conventions attracted more than five thousand students each year, and five hundred missionaries were sent out annually. One church historian credits the student movement with recruiting "a large proportion of the outstanding leaders in the world-wide spread of Protestant Christianity in the twentieth-century."[5] After 1920 the movement showed gradual decline.

Merton Strommen, founder of Search Institute of Minneapolis and one of the first research psychologists to focus on church ministry with youth, sees youth ministry as a movement growing primarily out of the past one hundred years. He sees three distinct eras through which we have moved and are now moving.

The Society Era
The society era began in the late 19th century as a response to the question, How can the church shelter and keep young people who have committed themselves to an active faith? An important answer emerged in 1881.

One February evening in Portland, Maine, the pastor of the Williston Congregational Church called his young people to the parsonage for cocoa and cookies. Clark presented to them an idea for a new organization. Even though he had to twist the arm of one youth before the others would follow, that meeting was to blossom into the International Christian Endeavor Society.[6]

Auxiliary groups known as leagues or societies blossomed everywhere. Their members devoted themselves to a variety of causes such as missions, temperance work, and music. National youth conventions, sometimes attracting 50,000 or more, were held.

Inadequacies in the society approach became apparent during the 1920s and the 1930s. Advocates of a new religious education philosophy criticized the society's separation from the denominations. They called for a unified, congregational-oriented youth ministry—an approach that could function inside the church and not as an auxiliary program.

The Fellowship Era
Oliver deWolf Cummings wrote: "Before the development of the Youth Fellowship, a state of affairs existed in the churches which was quite chaotic. Several organizations competed for the loyalty of youth with overlapping functions, gaps unprovided for, and with limited coordination."[7]

Gradually, the church discovered a simpler and more effective approach to its youth work. In one denomination after another, steps were taken to establish an improved organizational pattern—the Youth Fellowship. In these developments young people themselves, the leaders of youth, ministers, and national officials had a part.[8]

During the 1930s, Sunday evening fellowship meetings began to replace youth societies. These meetings were organized by the local congregation which began to take charge of all church-related youth activities. This massive shift in responsibility occurred in 39 major denominations and brought with it a change in the basic purpose of youth ministry, from nurturing the faith of young people to training them in churchmanship. It had the widespread support of clergy and congregational youth leaders.

Lasting from about 1935 to 1960, the fellowship era promoted leadership schools, caravans, Bible camps, and conventions with great success. In the late 1950s, however, many of the older youth began to drop out. Professional youth leaders began to criticize Sunday evening leadership meetings as paternalistic and irrelevant to the pressing needs of the day.

The Youth Ministry Era

This era had its roots in the early 1960s. Several things had become clear to church leaders.

"Young people have either been misjudged, misguided, or were emerging from their parents' social and political lethargy. They were looking for something more than fellowship groups. It also became evident that over-organization and competition needed to be reduced within youth ministries. Denominational leaders were questioning the segregation of youth from the over-all life of the church."[9]

The early days of the youth ministry era were marked by four trends:

• Stressing youth as full laity encouraged national youth organizations to disband.

• Stressing a youth ministry based on local needs discouraged denominational staffs from preparing programs for congregational use.

• Stressing person-centered ministries encouraged dropping the program approach of Sunday evening fellowships.

• Stressing youth ministry that is sensitive to human needs and injustice asked young people to become involved in social issues.

Unfortunately, this new movement had several weaknesses.

"Among most of the Protestant mainline denominations there was a dramatic dismantling of youth bureaus and services in the early 1960s. The aim was to integrate young people into the mainstream life of the church. Soon, however, dramatic issues were arising: civil rights, minority and third world needs, the Vietnam War and draft counseling, drugs, and the sexual revolution. Ministering to such demanding issues moved churches toward a concept and into an era of youth ministry almost without design."[10]

Southern Baptists were one of the few denominations that retained strong denominational support for youth ministry during this period. Support staff increased at the state and national level. Also, Southern Baptists were one of the few groups that retained a strong emphasis on the personal disciplines of the Christian life for youth. Merton Strommen noted, "It is my observation that in your church body [the Southern Baptist Convention], with its emphasis on a conversion theology, there was less slackening off during the 1960s and 1970s of emphases often soft-pedaled in other mainline denominations." Unfortunately, Southern Baptists may have underemphasized the response of Christian youth to pressing social issues.

The history of present-day Southern Baptist youth work (the past one hundred years) closely parallels the society era and the fellowship era. Bob Taylor has provided the following account.

The Southern Baptist Society Era
During the society era, in 1895, the Baptist Young People's Union (BYPU) was formed. The first national youth organization in the SBC, the BYPU sponsored area, state, and national meetings. It had slogans, theme songs, and even yells and cheers. Beginning as an organization for college-age youth, it quickly expanded to include high-school youth, as these individuals began to attend BYPU meetings with older brothers and sisters.

The Southern Baptist Fellowship Era
The success of BYPU in building strong Sunday evening programs for churches was a major factor precipitating the dawning of the second era, the fellowship era. With more and more

youth attending on Sunday nights, churches began planning af-ter-church fellowships. These fellowships offered youth extend-ed opportunities to visit and have fun with their friends.

These Sunday-night fellowships, still popular after almost one hundred years, were part of the initial activities sponsored for youth. From that simple, inconspicuous activity sprang the full-blown emphases we today call church recreation.

The fellowship era for Southern Baptists saw the youth work in churches grow from occasional Sunday night youth fellow-ships to a more varied menu of activities throughout the week.

Early in this era, a couple of highly significant events occurred which became major milestones in Southern Baptist youth work. In 1937, the Third Baptist Church in St. Louis, Missouri, called a person to work full-time as the church's "youth direc-tor." This is believed to be the first such action by any Southern Baptist church.

In 1938, the same church planned and conducted an event in which youth were spotlighted and given significant church lead-ership roles for a week. Logically called Youth Week, the event became the model for thousands of such weeks which were con-ducted in hundreds of churches over the following decades.

These two actions, the calling of a youth director and the be-ginning of Youth Week, touched off an avalanche of youth acti-vity. They launched a trend toward churches calling youth di-rectors. In a few years, hundreds of churches had called youth directors. By the 1950s it was almost commonplace for all large churches and many medium-sized churches to have secured a full-time or a part-time youth worker.

At least three observations can be made about this era—an era which was the forerunner of today's youth ministry:

Youth director and youth.—The arena of youth work during this era included primarily—and almost exclusively—the youth director and the youth. Little work was done with parents of youth or with ongoing youth workers.

The lack of consistent and frequent correlation and coordina-tion between the youth director and the youth workers created a serious flaw that still exists even today in some churches. It cre-ated a gap between the "youth program" planned by the youth director and the youth education work done by volunteer youth workers in the Sunday and Wednesday-evening youth education organizations.

Because of this characteristic of working mostly with youth, the term *youth director*, so popular during the 1940s and 1950s, seemed appropriate. Furthermore, other staff members were referred to by similar titles during the 1940s and 1950s—the education director, the music director, and the recreation director. The term *minister of youth* began to be more widely used and more descriptive in the 1960s.

The earlier struggles and victories of these other staff positions surely aided youth directors in a quest for ministry status. The move toward using the terms *minister of education* and *minister of music* in the 1950s made it easier later to use the term *minister of youth*. Today's ministers of youth should be grateful for the earlier work of other professional staff personnel. Their work made our pilgrimage for stature a bit smoother.

Youth activities.—The fellowship era was dominated by a project-to-project or an event-to-event kind of program. Youth work consisted mainly of a series of dated, sometimes disconnected, events. The calendar was full of ideas thought of by the youth director or suggested or done by another church across town or across the state.

Youth programs were made up mostly of recreational activities. This was the embryo of another significant emphasis among Southern Baptists. It developed something like this.

During the late 1930s, the 1940s, and the early 1950s, more and more churches were calling youth directors to direct a youth-activities program. Beginning as Sunday night fellowships, the program soon embraced all kinds of events, such as banquets, Friday-night game time, weekend retreats, and sporting events.

Before long churches began to realize that these exciting and fun events should not be limited to youth. Similar events began to be scheduled for children and adults. Since the youth director was the only one on the staff with experience in such undertakings, he or she usually planned these events.

This practice eventually became so widespread, and enough churches were by then calling recreation directors, that the Sunday School Board created the Church Recreation Department in 1954 to service this growing need. Like many staff positions, the recreation director began later to be referred to as the minister of recreation.

During this fellowship era a church's youth program was frequently evaluated by some congregations by how many, how big, and how exciting were the projects and activities conducted every week or month.

Adult-planned activities.—Not only was the youth program made up mainly of events and activities but also these activities were for the most part planned and directed by an adult. And that adult was usually the youth director.

The adults gave youth a banquet. They gave them a retreat, and they gave them a party. Youth came and sat and watched. With a few exceptions youth were not heavily involved in planning youth activities.

In the midst of this fellowship era, dominated by activities and adult-planned events, a small group of youth directors sensed a need for an approach that would penetrate the lives of youth primarily through a strong educational base rather than through exciting recreation. They felt that a gap between the youth program and the education work needed to be closed. They felt that the work of volunteer workers should be embraced under the banner of the church's total youth program.

There was—and is—nothing wrong with recreational activities. They provided—and do provide—a highly visible and attractive excitement that gave pizzazz to youth work in the 1930s, 1940s, and 1950s (and the 1960s, 1970s, and 1980s for that matter). Those exciting events and activities are still needed today. Without them, today's youth ministry would be sterile and bland. The secret is in the balance and the perspective.

On the center stage of youth work walked people like Helen May, Betty Jo Lacy, Roxie Jacobs, and Phil Harris. They began to ask why the youth program should not touch the family through parents and the other youth education organizations through the volunteer workers. These youth-related pioneers started a more balanced approach to youth work so that it eventually pulled youth work into youth ministry.

The Southern Baptist Youth Ministry Era

Strommen dates the youth ministry era from around 1960. That date, too, is fairly accurate for youth ministry in the SBC. The emerging concepts which began to show up in random locations in the 1940s and 1950s began to gain momentum in the 1960s. The phrase *youth ministry* grew in use, in concept, and in depth through the 1960s and the early 1970s.

In recognition of the growing trend and interest in youth education, Philip B. Harris was named in 1949 by the School of Religious Education at Southwestern Baptist Theological Seminary as the first Southern Baptist professor of youth education.

Prior to 1949, Joe Davis Heacock had taught a few courses in the general field of youth education. "I came to Southwestern Seminary to teach, among other things, a course in adolescent education, as we called it in those days," Heacock said in an interview. "But Philip Harris was the first full-time professor in youth education."

The Sunday School Board of the Southern Baptist Convention realized that the broadening field of youth ministry was gaining a foothold in churches of all sizes. Ministers of youth were working more and more with volunteer workers and with parents of youth. And while youth ministry was maintaining a high visibility with music and recreation, the base was broadening so as to cause it to rest heavily on an educational foundation.

In 1973, the Sunday School Board—under the direction of the Church Services and Materials Division Director Allen Comish—created the position of consultant in youth ministry coordination. This consultant was organizationally placed in the Church Administration Department. He works directly with ministers of youth, provides resources and supplies for these ministers, and seeks to help them understand their role more clearly. The creation of this new office symbolized recognition of the valuable staff position of minister of youth. Bob Taylor assumed this responsibility when it was begun in 1973 and served until 1984. Bob Taylor made a significant impact on Southern Baptist youth ministry. He found effective ways to crystallize and communicate broadly the concepts of a balanced, comprehensive ministry with youth.

Youth ministry, as we understand it today, is the flower blooming on the branches of the fellowship era, which in turn grew out of the roots of the society era.

Youth ministry is alive and well in the Southern Baptist Convention—one of the shining exceptions to the declining role of youth ministry in many denominations in the United States today.

Approximately one thousand ministers of youth serve in churches in the Southern Baptist Convention. This number represents full-time youth ministers with no combination assignments in their job description. No other denomination has even half that many ministers of youth.

When other professional church staff members who have youth ministry assignments in their combination job description are added to the number of youth-only personnel, the figure swells to more than eight thousand men and women in youth ministry-related staff positions. This total is more than all other denominations in the United States combined.

Counting all professional youth ministers and all part-time and volunteer youth ministry coordinators (approximately 3,000 in the latter group), 11,000 Southern Baptist churches have secured someone in a full-time, part-time, or volunteer basis to guide their youth ministries.

The fact that the six Southern Baptist theological seminaries are enjoying record enrollments is one evidence of the effectiveness of youth ministry in the life of Southern Baptist churches.

At a time when many denominations are continuing to cut back their national youth ministry staff, the Southern Baptist Convention has the largest number of youth-related, denominational professionals in its one-hundred-year history. Nearly fifty professionals work as editors, consultants, supervisors, artists, and professors in all Southern Baptist Convention agencies and institutions. No other denomination has more than fifteen professionals. Most have five to ten.

The combined educational, moral, and spiritual impact of Sunday School, Discipleship Training, youth music, Acteens, Pioneers, and High School Baptist Young Men on the life of a youth is probably unmatched in denominational history. Par ticular programs may have had stronger days in the past, but the total impact on youth of today's educational programs is extremely effective. The curriculum periodicals provided for youth by Southern Baptist agencies are the most attractive and most effective pieces available anywhere.

On average, Southern Baptist youth ministers are becoming older and more mature. In the 1950s and 1960s the great majority of youth directors were in their late teens or early twenties. Most planned to move into some other type of ministry before reaching their mid or late twenties.

By the late 1980s, the average age had increased to 33. A full 15 percent of full-time, part-time, and volunteer youth ministers were forty years of age or older.[11]

Effective youth ministry in the 1990s no longer requires a Pied Piper personality or an age close to members of the youth group. Age and maturity can be more of an asset than a liability. Recognizing this, contemporary youth ministers anticipate remaining in youth ministry an average of 16.5 more years.[12]

Southern Baptist youth ministers are also building longer tenures in individual churches. The average tenure among paid youth ministers is 3.6 years.[13] A decade or two ago this figure was only 18 months. Forty percent of contemporary youth ministers have been at a church four or more years. Most would agree that it takes two years to establish a strong foundation for ministry. During that time youth ministers are able to build significant relationships with staff members, key church leaders, teenagers, parents, and youth workers. Those deepening relationships produce trust, fellowship, support, and shared vision. Tenures longer than those two years are usually characterized by effective, rewarding ministry.

Youth ministry has come into its own as a significant vocational calling. At no time in modern history has this leader been more needed. And at no time has this leader been better prepared for the challenge.

---

[1]D. Campbell Wyckoff and Don Richter, eds., *Religious Education Ministry with Youth* (Birmingham, AL: Religious Education Press, 1982), 83.

[2]Ibid., 83-84.

[3]Dean Borgman, "A History of American Youth Ministry," *The Complete Book of Youth Ministry*, Warren S. Benson and Mark H. Senter III, eds. (Chicago: Moody, 1987), 62.

[4]Ibid., 63.

[5]Kenneth Scott Latourette, quoted in ibid., 64.

[6]Ibid., 64-65.

[7]Oliver deWolf Cummings, *The Youth Fellowship* (Valley Forge, PA: Judson Press, 1956), 16-17, quoted in ibid., 70.

[8]Ibid.

[9]Borgman, 71.

[10]Ibid.

[11]Research Services Department, "The Paid/Volunteer Status of Southern Baptist Convention Youth Coordinators" (Nashville: Sunday School Board of the Southern Baptist Convention, 1989), 13.

[12]Ibid., 18.

[13]Ibid., 16.

PERSONAL LEARNING ACTIVITIES

1. At what stage in history were youth first seen as a distinct group?

2. Compare the society era, the fellowship era, and the youth ministry era.

3. How were these periods in other denominations similar to or different from those of Southern Baptists?

4. When did a Southern Baptist church first call a paid staff member to work with youth?

5. Describe the shift from youth director to minister of youth.

CHAPTER 2

THE MINISTER OF YOUTH'S CALLING AND CHARACTERISTICS

The Calling

The past few years have been traumatic for me as a youth minister. Three especially significant events compelled me to reexamine my ministry.

First, my oldest daughter became a teenager. I could feel eyes all across our community looking at me to see how I would handle the adolescent storms anticipated in my own home. Was my counsel really practical, or was it unrealistic and outdated?

Second, another ministry offer forced me to decide whether to remain directly involved in a ministry with young people or after twenty years to chart my ministry in another direction.

Third, I reached the age of 40. New youth in our group didn't know whether to put a Mr. in front of my name. And when I attended youth

Dennis M. Rogers
Associate director
Church Training
Department
Georgia Baptist
Convention
Atlanta, Georgia

ministry conferences, I was addressed as "sir" by my peers. To be honest, much of the programming I had done over the years no longer seemed as attractive. Activities such as lockins and days at amusement parks took their toll physically more quickly than they once did. I also found myself short-circuiting effective communication processes in relating to youth by being more judgmental and critical of their actions and attitudes. I knew beyond any shadow of doubt that I had been divinely directed into a ministry with youth years earlier. The question now was whether I was being directed away from this ministry because of my age or for other reasons. My desire was to remain obedient to God's call whether as a youth minister or in some other ministry capacity.

A Remembered Call

I sensed a need to recollect my earlier call to youth ministry. Remembering how God had guided my life then might help give me direction now. My call into youth ministry had been gradual. God had used circumstances and opportunities as they had occurred to take me a step at a time to the role of vocational youth minister. The journey had included part-time youth ministry, then secular employment followed by combined secular employment and youth ministry. Secular employment gave way to a theological education.

Through this process God revealed His will for me. In retrospect I can see the process as a preparatory time full of learning experiences. I can also see the process as one in which I experienced a growing sense of peace and fulfillment in my spirit which confirmed the rightness of the decision I had made. Other colleagues have shared with me the circumstances of their calls; each is different.

God directs lives in many varied ways. Some calls are spontaneous and dramatic. Others are the result of God's using people to encourage others. Some colleagues shared with me that their commitment to youth ministry was just a natural step. It never occurred to them that they could be involved in any other ministry. Although God uses many different methods in calling people into the ministry, the reality of the call is the same.

As I reviewed my past ministry experiences, I remembered those significant events that God used to mold my ministry with youth. Some experiences were high moments such as seeing one of my young people respond to a ministry call or feeling personally affirmed or honored in a special way. At other times I was painfully aware of how I had failed to minister to a hurting youth, youth parent, or fellow youth worker. God used both types of experiences to teach me and to create a ministry style in me that He desired.

I came to understand more fully that God's call to an individual to serve Him in a vocational ministry will be accompanied by His gifting the individual to minister effectively. Richard Ross beautifully stated that truth in this way: "God chose you [me] from all others to serve your church because of a unique constellation of your gifts, your church's needs, etc. It is a mistake to compare yourself, your gifts, and the success of your ministry to others. Find your worth in God's call."[1]

Even though God's call to individuals varies, some characteristics are common to every call to youth ministry. These can help determine God's guidance. I discovered four characteristics in recollecting my call which renewed my ministry and gave me insight into God's continued call in my life.

God's call to youth ministry must be a call to continue one's own spiritual pilgrimage.—This applies to all Christians but especially to those called to vocational ministry. Sadly, however, because ministers of youth work with youth and even adults who may be theologically less educated, all too often they curtail their own spiritual journey, relying on what they understand and have experienced in the past. To minister effectively with youth and encourage their spiritual growth demands that the youth minister remain fresh in spiritual experiences and encounters with God. The desire for fresh experiences with God should be ever growing, and we should arrange our lives for such experiences.

God's call to minister with youth is always accompanied by an unconditional love for them.—Loving and accepting youth only after they become Christians, or a member of your youth group, or after they cease certain wrong activities will reflect a distorted view of God's love and may hamper attempts to reach youth. God gifts His ministers to love unconditionally.

God's call to youth ministry is evidenced by a commitment of time and emotion.—Youth ministers cannot be detached. To love unconditionally means being vulnerable. Youth as well as adults take advantage of a loving, sensitive spirit. Youth ministers must realize that their emotions will run the gambit because of the joys and sorrows youth encounter and, therefore, they encounter. Time cost is significant; and while other relationships and responsibilities take priority, the youth minister willingly accepts a schedule that involves sacrifice.

Ministers of youth discover that being with youth energizes their spirits.—This is also one way God confirms a continued call to minister with youth. While physically, mentally, and emotionally fatigued, youth ministers may still find that their spirits are ignited by involvement with young people.

These four characteristics can be sign posts in determining God's call into youth ministry because all are essential if a ministry with youth is to be long-term and effective.

This special call to minister to and with teenagers, parents, and workers is part of a broader call to vocational ministry itself. Most children and youth begin to sense God's call into ministry years before they clarify the specific arena in which they will work. Both churches and staff members should recognize that youth ministers are true ministers who have committed their lives to a significant area of church life.

A Renewed Call

Realizing that these four characteristics were still active in my life led me to renew my commitment to God's call to work with youth, their parents, and other youth workers. While my age certainly affected some ministry activities, I came to realize that my age and experience offered more assets than liabilities. I decided that whatever difficulty I felt I had experienced in effectively communicating with my youth was due to factors other than my age. Actually I have more patience and insight as a result of my age and experience which is a valuable asset in my ministry.

Today men and women can remain in vocational youth ministry positions much easier than they could have years earlier because of a new understanding of youth ministry by many churches. Not too many years ago the youth minister or youth director was called by a church primarily to provide a program of recreational and educational activities.

Today the role of the minister of youth is understood to be more than just an activities director. Now youth ministers are called to coordinate a comprehensive ministry to and with youth.

Extended tenure should be the norm instead of the exception because only through time can relationships be developed and nurtured, resulting in ministry opportunities to young people and their families and friends. Those who have endured ministry pains and remained in one church for several years have discovered a multitude of counseling opportunities with youth and their parents. This ministry is possible because the necessary trust has been established.

To remain in a church ministry position long enough to see youth through adolescence means opportunities to influence them significantly. The mature minister of youth discovers by experience that the most effective ministry is done within the context of relationships rather than through programming.

Mature ministers of youth can more easily discover that time spent directly with youth should encompass approximately one third of their schedule and energy. Their ministry is also strengthened and multiplied by relating to, nurturing and equipping both parents of youth and other adults who work with youth. Building relationships with adults can also provide a strong network of support and encouragement for the difficult days of ministry.

Including parents, other adults, and youth in the planning process may cause some to question the leadership of the ministry. Who is the governing authority responsible for ministry with the youth of a local church? In recent years new terminology beautifully expresses the answer to this question. The term is *shared ministry*. *Shared ministry* means that no one person has the unrealistic task of providing programming and ministry for the young people of the church. The responsibility is shared by those youth and adults who are involved in the ministry.

The Youth Ministry Council has been developed to provide the philosophy and methodology for youth, parents, other youth workers, and related church staff personnel to participate in planning and implementing the church's ministry to youth.[2] Today experienced workers with youth do not have to question their vocational call to ministry simply because of advancing age. Often with age comes wisdom and experience that can add stability and credibility to ministry. Evangelism becomes a priority. Time spent only with youth is amended to include parents and other adult workers. Activities built around the minister of youth are replaced by an emphasis on strengthening ongoing church programming. The mature youth minister uses recreation to support the work of the organizations and as a ministry vehicle.The equipping and affirming of these programs with committed youth workers can add balance, enthusiasm, and a shared vision of the joys and tasks of youth ministry.

The Character

When I think of character traits needed to be an effective minister of youth, I think about the delightful children's story by Robert N. Munsch entitled *The Paper Bag Princess*. Elizabeth, a beautiful princess with expensive clothes, is engaged to marry a prince named Ronald. One day a dragon comes while Ronald and Elizabeth are together at her castle. The dragon burns her castle with his fiery breath and carries off Prince Ronald. Not only is Elizabeth's castle burned but also all of her clothes. Elizabeth decides to chase the dragon and get Ronald back. The only thing she finds to wear is a paper bag. She tracks down the dragon, cleverly outwits him, and rescues Ronald from his prison. Ronald looks at Elizabeth and says:

"Elizabeth, you are a mess! You smell like ashes, your hair is all tangled, and you are wearing a dirty old paper bag. Come back when you are dressed like a real princess."

"Ronald", said Elizabeth, "your clothes are really pretty and your hair is very neat. You look like a real prince, but you are a bum."

"They didn't get married after all."[3]

The youth minister does not need to be overly concerned about external things, such as wearing fashionable clothes, driving a flashy car, being able to play the guitar, or telling funny jokes. The minister's values are important. What convictions guide his life? What is the minister with youth really like when troubled times and crises come?

No one effective personality type characterizes a minister of youth. Different people, described in different ways with different personalities, can meaningfully relate and minister to the needs of young people. Some common character traits, however, should mark the man or woman who is helping to shape the lives of youth. A good ministry model is found in Paul's first letter to the church at Thessalonica:

> You know, brothers, that our visit to you was not a failure. We had previously suffered and been insulted in Philippi, as you know, but with the help of our God we dared to tell you his gospel in spite of strong opposition. For the appeal we make does not spring from error or impure motives, nor are we trying to trick you. On the contrary, we speak as men approved by God to be entrusted with the gospel. We are not trying to please men but God, who tests our hearts. You know we never used flattery, nor did we put on a mask to cover up greed—God is our witness. We were not looking for praise from men, not from you or anyone else.
>
> As apostles of Christ we could have been a burden to you, but we were gentle among you, like a mother caring for her little children. We loved you so much that we were delighted to share with you not only the gospel of God but our lives as well, because you had become so dear to us. Surely you remember, brothers, our toil and hardship; we worked night and day in order not to be a burden to anyone while we preached the gospel of God to you.
>
> You are witnesses, and so is God, of how holy, righteous and blameless we were among you who believed. For you know that we dealt with each of you as a father deals with his own children, encouraging, comforting and urging you to live lives worthy of God, who calls you into his kingdom and glory (1 Thess. 2:1-12).[4]

The first character trait Paul described is *conviction*. He said that with God's help he dared to share the gospel even though others opposed him. Convictions are those unshakable and undeniable values that guide our lives without question of compromise no matter how costly. Too many of us are more prone to live life based on preferences instead of convictions. *Preferences* could be defined as desiring the right things but lacking the strength to follow through if the price is too great. Effective ministers of youth must develop strong convictions about what is of utmost value in their beliefs and behavior. Their modeling of the Christian life based on internal convictions will influence more youth than any programming or lecture.

Second, Paul spoke of *integrity* when he said that his motives were pure and that he was not trying to trick the Thessalonians. Furthermore, he had been approved by God to be entrusted with his ministry; therefore, he was trying to please God, not people.

Integrity for ministers of youth has many implications. Perhaps the most important is that they do what they do for the right reason—to please God. Youth ministers, like other leaders, face strong temptation to do certain things simply to earn the approval and applause of significant others both in our personal lives and in our ministry. The goal above all else for the minister of youth should be to please God in all that is thought, said, and done. *Integrity* also implies that, although certain methods or activities may be enticing and may provide short-term benefits, any questionable or deceptive ways are avoided at all costs.

Paul also described his ministry as one of *gentleness*. He said that he was like a mother caring for her little children. Gentleness almost has a negative connotation for some men and women, implying weakness; but gentleness is a strong character trait. A person who is truly gentle practices self-control and is able to handle adverse situations and injustices calmly and positively. The minister of youth who fails to respond to others with tenderness and mercy forfeits many ministry opportunities. The youth minister who practices gentleness when another behavior is expected earns the respect of young people.

The next character trait we discover in this letter is *love*. A minister's love for youth is unconditional. Caring and ministry continue no matter what a youth does or says. This kind of love is not generated by one's own strength but is expressed by the Holy Spirit within the person. He enables us to demonstrate love even to those who reject the greatest Love.

Next Paul said he worked day and night not to be a burden to anyone. For ministers of youth today, that translates into being industrious. Ministering to the needs of youth and their parents as well as equipping other adults to do the same often requires long, hard hours. Being industrious means that ministers of youth do not resort to questionable shortcuts but instead are willing to do whatever is necessary to minister effectively.

Some churches view youth ministers as persons who spend all of their time just "hanging out" with the youth. Previous staff members may have left such an impression. Youth ministers today manage their time in a professional manner. They are responsible with office hours, and they follow through on assignments. Establishing professional credibility when first arriving at a church should be a high priority. Responsible use of time in the early weeks sets a tone for years to come.

Paul described his conduct among the Thessalonians as being *holy*, *righteous*, and *blameless*. These admirable characteristics are essential for a minister of youth to be effective. Ministry with youth is done within the context of relationships more than within the context of activities. Young people are impacted more by the character and life of adults who work with them than by what they say. Persons who are holy, righteous, and blameless have a distinctive life-style and value system that sets them apart from the mainstream of society.

While the youth of this generation have generally chosen financial gain as a measure for success, they are acutely aware of those rare people who have found a higher quality of life. Ministers of youth influence youth by their character and by their commitment to Jesus Christ.

This kind of life can result only from the minister's own growing spiritual pilgrimage. Too often the demands of ministry have crowded out the best intentions to worship God daily. No number of sermons preached, Bible studies taught, or retreats led can substitute for this ministry prerequisite.

How can a youth minister lead others to make quiet time a

priority when the youth minister hasn't made it one. In this daily time God renews and reminds us that His presence in our lives enables us to find confidence and meaning. We can experience His intended peace and joy.

One way a youth minister can aid the quest for intimacy with God is to find another person with whom to share spiritual growth and concerns. A spiritual friend is committed to another's spiritual wholeness. Spiritual friends encourage our spiritual growth by their intercessory praying, by sharing insights from their own spiritual pilgrimage, by modeling Christian maturity and responsibility, and by mutually agreeing to be accountable for Christian life-style disciplines.[5]

Sadly, a growing character problem among adults who work with youth is sexual immorality. That kind of behavior inflicts all kinds of emotional trauma, destroys any opportunity to foster spiritual growth, and creates suspicion toward other youth workers who have pure motives. Too many ministers of youth feel that they can handle sexually provocative movies, television programs, and magazines without being personally affected. They put themselves in compromising situations with youth of the opposite sex and succumb to the temptation of giving and receiving unhealthy expressions of affection. Some even bolster their egos by seeing if they can physically attract their young people. God's call to men and women to invest their lives in ministry with youth is a call to moral purity. This distinctive lifestyle is maintained by a daily worship time with God and by carefully avoiding situations that might lead to conduct or activities which may be seen by others as questionable.

Ministers of youth also face a crisis of ethical integrity. Some businessmen who have dealt professionally with youth ministers have stated that they have been difficult to work with and dishonest in their business transactions. The following is excerpted from a letter from an owner of a retreat center:

> Some youth ministers have demonstrated lack of integrity by (1) reporting and paying for fewer people than they actually bring; (2) making reservations and not canceling them when they cancel the retreat; (3) making reservations, signing a contract, canceling the retreat then refusing to

pay cancellation fees agreed upon in the contract; (4) lying about financial arrangements made with the retreat center to their church and to thei r adult counselors; (5) mismanaging church money by spending church money for personal items.

Moral purity and integrity ought never to come into question in describing those men and women who have been given the privilege and responsibility of spiritually nurturing young people. Jesus' words in Matthew's Gospel ought to be an ever-present guard against any conduct that might deter the spiritual maturation of those with whom they minister: "But if anyone causes one of these little ones who believe in me to sin, it would be better for him to have a large millstone hung around his neck and to be drowned in the depths of the sea" (Matt. 18:6, NIV).

The last description of his character among the Thessalonians that Paul gave is that he was like a father relating to his own children, encouraging, comforting, and urging them to live in a way that is pleasing to God. Carroll Freeman, a professor at New Orleans Baptist Theological Seminary, labeled such conduct as "therapeutic personhood." Therapeutic personhood is another way of saying that one has a way of relating to others that enables others to feel better when they are in that person's presence. Certainly such a description ought to fit ministers of youth because they work with a group of people who constantly question their self-worth. Youth need to be around people who in the right way will help them feel better.

Youth ministers ought to be characterized by a life-style that demonstrates concern and care for the youth and adults with whom they minister. The ability to make every person in a group feel special and important is a tremendous ministry asset.

How can this ability be cultivated? The youth minister needs to spend a significant amount of time building and nurturing relationships with youth, parents of youth, and other adults involved in the youth ministry. That is foundational.

This may be accomplished in small ways.

● The youth minister might choose to call or send cards to all youth and youth workers on their birthdays.

● In addition the minister of youth should be aware of meaningful events in the lives of youth, parents of youth, and workers and respond appropriately with notes, calls, and visits.

● A strategy to visit youth in their surroundings and have them in various groups in the youth minister's home can greatly assist the personalization process.

● Affirming and encouraging a youth's strengths in different ways can lead to a bonding that opens the door to opportunities to instruct and encourage in areas of weakness. Encouragement and affirmation of others should not be a coincidental comment rarely heard from the lips of the minister with youth but rather a part of a life-style that challenges youth, parents, and other adults to be actively concerned about the well-being of others.

The most important thought about developing "therapeutic personhood" is that it begins, grows, and is maintained by prayer. The minister of youth who consistently encourages others outwardly has also been interceding for them before God. Specific and daily intercessory prayer for others should mark the ministry of the men and women who work with youth. A prayer journal reminding the youth worker of the strengths and needs of individual youth, their parents, and other adult workers can be a vital ministry tool.

The minister with youth will have many opportunities to structure youth programming in order to be in the limelight. Although ministers of youth may sometimes need to take the forefront and assume a commanding position, their motivation always ought to be leading by serving—being willing to do the menial to model servanthood. Those whose desire is to be recognized by God for a job well done and not by persons for some accomplishment will most impact the lives of youth, their parents, and coworkers. A servant spirit may not always make an impression, but it will always make a difference.

---

[1]Quoted in Larry McGuire, "The Youth Minister's Leaving and Beginning Again," *The Personal World of the Minister of Youth*, Richard Ross, compiler (Nashville: Convention Press, 1988), 114.

[2]For more information see Richard Ross, *Youth Ministry Council Handbook* (Nashville: Convention Press, 1987).

[3]Robert N. Munsch, *The Paper Bag Princess* (Toronto: Annick Press,

Ltd., 1980), 21-23.

[4]From the Holy Bible, *New International Version*, copyright © 1973, 1989, 1984 by International Bible Society. Subsequent quotations are marked NIV.

[5]For more help in deepening your own walk with God, see Jerome Smith, "The Youth Minister's Spiritual Fitness," *The Personal World of the Minister of Youth*, comp. Richard Ross (Nashville: Convention Press, 1988).

PERSONAL LEARNING ACTIVITIES

1. What four characteristics are common to the call of most ministers of youth?

2. How has the changed view of the role of the minister of youth encouraged persons to stay in this ministry for a longer time?

3. What qualities does Paul mention in 1 Thessalonians 12:1-12 that apply to ministers of youth?

CHAPTER 3

THE MINISTER OF YOUTH'S PREPARATION AND EDUCATION

"To be, or not to be: that is the question." Trained, that is! This question is often asked by the prospective minister of youth. We are not too far removed from an untrained clergy in America among some evangelical groups. Unfortunately some still think that training is unnecessary. This attitude comes from some who believe that God-called individuals are equipped as called. Others believe that youth ministry is a field that does not require training but talent and a desire to be with youth.

One of my most disappointing experiences was when a teacher I deeply respected revealed his limited understanding and expressed the sentiment that training for youth ministry wasn't necessary and that anyone could do it! If he were still living, I would make every attempt to correct this idea. Interestingly, most of those who espouse this position are

Philip H. Briggs
Professor of youth and recreation
Southwestern Baptist Theological Seminary
Fort Worth, Texas

youthful and enthusiastic but just do not understand the situation. Often these same highly motivated individuals feel they do not have time to waste in training.

To think that youth who change so much during their teen years would not need the best of instruction and guidance is ironic. Molding the lives of youth can be an overwhelming challenge. When one teaches, the future is not only touched but determined.

Far too many churches look upon youth ministry as strictly an activity-oriented task. While activities play a vital part in youth lives, they are not the only experiences needed. Because of the pliability of adolescents, their mentors need expert training and maturity. During the last 15 years I have asked groups of youth leaders to recall the name and age of the adult, other than their parents, who made the greatest contribution to their lives when they were teenagers. At least 85 percent of every group named adults over 30.

Everyone has two ages, physiological and psychological. The latter is the critical one with those who work in youth ministry. Those who feel they may be too old for youth ministry may mistakenly think they are to be identical to youth, when the real test of effective leadership is being able to identify with them. Ministers of children are not expected to resign when they reach 30, why then should the youth minister?

Many effective school teachers and administrators spend their entire careers guiding youth. As youth ministers age, life circumstances change. However, every person faces these adjustments and continues in a chosen vocation. Why should the youth minister be expected to be different?

If a person enters youth ministry to fulfill ego needs, the position will only remain attractive as long as these needs are met. Some do grow out of the position. Most tragic is the youth minister at 30 who is still searching and remains an adolescent.

Three factors maintain stability in youth ministry—calling, training, and continuing education. Chapter 2 deals with the call. Suffice it to say that one's call to youth ministry is the only thing that keeps one at the task. Preparation and training are the next major ingredients for success and stability.

Training or education in a general sense is not the only challenge. A call to serve is a call to prepare. A good Christian is also to be a good student. Loving the Lord means to love Him with the heart and mind. Jesus challenged His followers with the greatest commandment, to love the Lord your God with all your heart, soul, strength, and mind (see Mark 12:28-30).

Youth ministers can be witnesses as they achieve academic greatness and mature into middle adulthood, too. God can so beautifully use a skilled instrument to a greater degree to reach, touch, and guide youth. We should prepare to serve our Lord. One's training for ministry is both informal and formal.

Informal Education

The aspiring youth minister should recognize that serving faithfully in a local church is a must. Being a volunteer in mission projects and children's work while remaining an active member of a youth group is essential. This includes worship, Bible study, and discipleship training.

High-school youth can find good opportunities for training by working with older children and junior-high youth. Youth Week and other hands-on experiences contribute to preparation. Many churches encourage youth participation on some church committees. This experience is valid training. Experience is gained in more ways than having a salary.

College and seminary students not on church staffs should actively pursue opportunities for service with youth. Many churches are willing to enlist young adults as Youth Sunday School teachers, Discipleship Training leaders, missions education workers, or youth music leaders.

Church search committees looking for youth ministers frequently ask about candidates' volunteer work with youth. They want to know if one's commitment to teenagers goes beyond receiving a paycheck.

An increasing number of churches are calling youth ministry interns. College or seminary students serve part-time under the leadership of the minister of youth. Interns make a valuable contribution to the churches they serve, and they receive significant on-the-job education.

Formal education is expanding, too. Forty years ago the high-school diploma was adequate education for most jobs. What the high-school diploma was then, the bachelor's degree is today. Soon, the master's degree may be the least amount of formal education needed. Every potential youth minister should plan beyond high school to attend both college and seminary.

Preparation includes skill development. To prepare for youth ministry, a person might look for opportunities to gain education or experience in the following areas.

- Ability to keep four or five youth program organizations functioning effectively.
- Ability to understand and minister to the complex problems facing parents of youth.
- Ability to handle hundreds or thousands of dollars of budget funds responsibly.
- Ability to counsel youth in a variety of complex problem areas.
- Ability to handle the Scriptures without violating principles of biblical interpretation.
- Ability to communicate effectively with a variety of audiences both verbally and through the printed page.
- Ability to do long- and short-range planning, and the ability to implement those plans.
- Ability to use sports and recreation as components in a balanced program of ministry.
- Ability to function well with a multiple staff, complex office operations, and numerous committee relationships.
- Ability to train and inspire adults to perform a ministry to youth through their elected positions.[1]

Titles are important because they create images in the minds of church members. Historically the term *youth director* was used in churches to designate the adult who guided youth. Through the influence of Philip B. Harris, the first full-time professor of youth education in the SBC, the position was given vocational identity. This happened with an expanded curriculum on the seminary level, but its influence was felt in the churches. This expanded concept opened the opportunity to look upon the position with greater respect and influence. Along with this change came the need for ministry to, with, and for youth.

Ministry to parents of youth developed in the 1970s as a new horizon for youth ministry. An untrained youth minister may find difficulty in ministering to parents of youth. Respect is an earned quality that is the basis for effective ministry. Youth ministers gain trust with parents by planning well, spending budget money responsibly, and returning to the church parking lot after a youth trip at the published arrival time.

Undoubtedly, as the needs of youth and their culture emerged in the 1960s and 1970s, pastoral roles were filled by youth directors. An unfortunate title has emerged of late, *the youth pastor*. This designation is most common in nondenominational and evangelical churches. It is a misnomer since the adult who works with youth is not the pastor of the church but one who ministers to youth. Youth ministers do, of course, have pastoral responsibilities to youth, but they are not pastors. The staff member who ministers to the youth of a church should complement the work of the pastor, not seek to supplant the pastor.

College and Seminary

Major decisions face the high-school graduate—what college to attend, what major to pursue, and how to pay for the education. Selecting a college demands study and evaluation, facing such questions as kind of college, accreditation, course offerings, faculty, and track record of their graduates.

One's formal education needs to have goals for the future beyond the credentials of a degree. Course selections, degree plans, majors and minors all need careful consideration.

Since seminary education will be the goal for most youth ministers, should a college major be in Bible or religious education? Should a college degree for ministry build a base for a master's degree, or should college courses be in liberal arts as a broad base with specialization following in seminary? Each student should consider these questions carefully.

Skills can be developed with an appropriate curriculum including the following areas of training:

1. Bible, evangelism, church history, philosophy of religion-,and theology.

2. Developmental psychology of youth and middle adults.

3. Management: staff relations, time, supervision, training of volunteers, budget and purchasing, organizing, and planning.

4. Counseling: personal crises, issue oriented, and peer.

5. Communication, public relations, and advertising.

6. Recreation: social, outdoor, athletics, arts, crafts, music, first aid, and physical fitness.

7. Religious education: grouping, grading, educational psychology (teaching/learning), foundations and design for curriculum, and missions education.

8. Parenting.

9. Church music.

The serious student will examine the areas of need and recognize that ministry to youth is like marriage; it is not to be entered into lightly.

Some aspirants think that content of the above subjects is all that is needed and ignore vital skill development. During my college days a new football coach was hired. He had had an illustrious career in college as an all-American as well as an all-pro. But he was a failure as a coach. He could not teach! This can also be the pitfall of young, enthusiastic youth ministers.

Knowing the Bible and related subjects is important; but the ability to teach, guide, and communicate these truths into the experience of youth is also necessary. Good biblical content may suffer if the youth minister as teacher has little knowledge of lesson planning, aims, and outcomes. One pastor called asking advice for his young youth minister after a near riot at a junior-high retreat. During a two-hour private meditation period, the junior-high youth in their boredom became extremely restless. A fisticuff broke out, and a near tragedy occurred. The youth minister was an eager, zealous theologian who had good ideas but was totally unaware of the psychological needs of young adolescents. His training was inadequate.

Youth ministers should have seminary education. The maturation seminary students experience is incalculable! This observation is based on my 24 years of teaching in two seminaries and watching students discover themselves as well as their vocational identity while in a seminary. They also realize that the seminary is a finding place, not a finishing school.

The college degree should be a broad liberal degree giving the students the best possible education. The major in Bible or religious education is not the only option. Recreation, education, music, business, or other majors may be of interest to a potential youth minister. Certainly, survey cources in Bible and other courses in religion could be taken as preparatory for seminary.

Another reason for a seminary degree is the pragmatic realization that churches look to the seminaries for prospective staff members. Many college graduates are disillusioned when they cannot secure a position in a church with their college diploma alone.

Should a student pursue the master of divinity or the master of arts in religious education degree in seminary? No one can say what every student should do. Which degree to pursue is a personal decision based on how the student feels God's is leading. Either degree has built-in advantages of electives that should be wisely chosen. These electives should certainly include courses especially designed to train students in youth ministry. Not everyone has the aptitude to be effective in youth ministry, and the challenge demands specialized training.

Masters' degrees at a seminary are not like the master's degrees from colleges. The master's degree from seminary assumes that a number of hours needed to secure the degree include an undergirding of studies in seminary. This is why the master of divinity degree is 92 hours and the master of arts in religious education is 68 hours. The average college master's degree is 2540 hours.

Which seminary should be attended for preparation in youth ministry? Begin by asking God to lead you to the campus of His choice. All schools have advantages and disadvantages. What are your goals? What course offerings are available? Some offer only one or two courses in some areas, while others have majors or minors in those same areas. Become acquainted with some seminary graduates. Don't limit yourself to pastors, but do consult them. Visit the campus and interview the faculty members who teach youth ministry courses as well as other subjects. Read articles and books written by the professors. Consider visiting the churches of youth ministers whom you consider good role models. Seek to get the broadest education possible. Consider the theological beliefs of the seminary, but don't be afraid of being challenged and stretched.

Recently, I surveyed 50 incoming seminary students who are majoring in youth ministry. In their written responses to this question, "Why have you chosen to attend seminary for training in youth ministry?" several patterns emerged. Here are several statements that represented the major thrust of their responses. These may be helpful to you while considering seminary as a place of preparation for youth ministry.

"I felt I needed the best training possible to minister effectively to youth."

"Seminary seems the best place to develop the relationships with others who are going into youth ministry."

"Churches need youth ministers that have a solid theological knowledge. . . . Seminary will prepare me."

"I felt the leadership of the Holy Spirit to do this."

"Seminary education is essential."

"I will be shaping their lives. . . . [I feel] called of God to youth ministry."

"Because God has given me some talents to work with youth and I want to develop these."

"I have been serving as a youth minister in a church. . . . I have found that there are so many issues and dilemmas that I am not equipped to handle. Also seminary will help me to be an adequate teacher for youth . . . and will also help me in my growth as a Christian."

"I have chosen seminary so that I can gain knowledge from trained and experienced teachers."

"I love youth! I need help!"

"A seminary degree will be helpful in securing a full-time church."

"The men I admire most in my life have come from seminary."

"To sharpen my skills, educate myself to various Southern Baptist programs."

"I strongly believe God has called me to minister to youth and their families. Unless I hear otherwise, I desire to do this the rest of my life."

"Because if I don't learn the right way to do it, I'll end up wasting valuable time and energy."

"Youth ministry is not a stepping-stone to something [else] for me . . . therefore, with such an important calling, I feel a need and have a desire to be the best possible leader."

Continuing Education

Continuing education is a challenge every youth minister must meet. Continuing education for any minister is vital to fulfillment and effectiveness. Those who leave ministry list burnout and frustration as factors contributing to their seeking another profession. Both of these crises can be avoided, at least in part, by continued learning and growth. A well-planned program of personal growth and further training can help to stem the tide of dropouts from youth ministry.

This need can be met as simply as maintaining personal study habits. One early mistake new graduates make is to say, "Wow, no more books!" How unwise! If a respite is needed, make it short-term. Design a personal study plan to expand your mind and heart! Would you seek medical doctors or lawyers who have not kept abreast of their fields? Why should ministers be any different?

Make time for study in your weekly schedule. Collect and read books, journals, and newsletters to stay current on youth issues.[2] Read and recommend materials to youth leaders with whom you work! It will inspire and encourage them. This conduct will also model good leadership style. Your youth leaders will never exceed the example set before them. Effective youth ministers also know and read regularly the denominational curriculum pieces published for youth leaders in the churches.

Most communities have educational television or cable networks that offer early morning instruction classes. Public schools and community colleges offer adult education programs at a reasonable cost that could benefit the minister. Videotape rental companies are developing self-help units for the general public. Public libraries are willing to assist citizens in developing a reading program from their holdings or through book exchange and rental policies.

Continuing education plans also need to include conferences and workshops. Attending those of your denomination are essential. Meetings offered by other groups may also have value.[3]

Develop friendships with youth ministers of other denominations. Public- and private-school educators are another strong source of help and improvement. Stay close to youth, know what they are reading and experiencing.

Also read beyond the field of youth ministry. Recreational reading benefits intellectual growth and freshness. A pastor friend moved across the nation to a new church and immediately began to read the history of his new state and region. It wasn't long until this material found its way into messages to the delight of the congregation.

Personal Fitness

Although physical fitness is not continuing education as such, it is a necessary ingredient in maintaining good mental health. Youth ministry is a stress-filled position. Doing the job adequately will mean taking on some of the stress of the youth and their parents. Physical exercise helps eliminate stress and provides one of the best times to think, plan, and wrestle with decisions and actions to be taken.

Regular days off and annual vacation periods are essential to good health. The job is always there when the time away is complete. Ministers who feel that their work can't get along without them may be taking themselves too seriously.

Maintain your personal time for you and your family. In the scheme of God's plan, mate precedes ministry!

All youth ministers dream of developing a discipleship program among the youth of the church but sometimes forget to maintain their own days with the Lord and the Scriptures. You cannot teach that which you do not know any more than you can come back from where you haven't been! So it is with developing disciples. Our Lord began a close personal relationship with the Heavenly Father as a 12-year-old and maintained that relationship throughout His life. Jesus' closeness to God was so apparent to the twelve that they asked Him to teach them to pray and to show them the Father! Jesus' devotional life is the model for the youth minister who will be an example to youth.

A prayer list for personal use can enhance intelligent praying and strengthen one's faith as answers are given and understood. Few youth groups meet without requests for prayers being stated by concerned youth.

Maintain a sense of humor! Those without a sense of humor may lack the sense to live a healthy, productive life. Youth work can take its toll on your psyche perhaps as nothing else can; but with a grin, the grit of life can be met and overcome. Ecclesiastes, the resident pessimist of the Old Testament, declared that life's balance includes all dimensions of living, including laughter.

Youth ministry is a worthy calling. Youth, parents, and workers need and deserve a leader who is prepared and who is continuing to grow and develop.

---

[1]Richard Ross, "The Minister of Youth: Calling, Qualification, and Preparation," *The Work of the Minister of Youth*, comp. Bob R. Taylor (Nashville: Convention Press, 1982), 28-29.

[2]For a current list of significant youth ministry books, write to Richard Ross, 127 Ninth Avenue, North, Nashville, Tennessee 37234.

[3]For more information concerning coming youth ministry conferences, write Richard Ross, 127 Ninth Avenue, North, Nashville, Tennessee 37234.

PERSONAL LEARNING ACTIVITIES

1. What abilities can a person develop to aid in youth ministry?

2. Give three reasons a youth minister should get a seminary education.

3. What kinds of things should a youth minister read for continuing education?

CHAPTER 4

THE MINISTER OF YOUTH'S PHILOSOPHY OF YOUTH MINISTRY

A philosophy of youth ministry is similar to the human skeleton. It gives shape and form to ministry. A body with no skeleton could never move forward in a purposeful way. Neither can a youth ministry with no underlying philosophy. A body without a skeleton is just a collection of parts. A youth ministry without a philosophy is just a collection of events.

Compared to the beauty of a healthy body, a skeleton seems dull and uninteresting. Compared to the excitement of creative youth programming, examining one's philosophy seems mundane. And yet neither an attractive body nor purposeful programming is possible without a solid structure.

Most youth ministers have chosen one of four youth ministry models. Three of the models contain several valid strengths but even more weaknesses. The fourth model seems to

Richard Ross
Youth ministry
consultant
Church
Administration
Department
Sunday School Board
Nashville, Tennessee

offer the best underlying structure for effective youth ministry. Each model deserves examination.

The "Let Me Do It" Model

Parents of two-year-olds often hear them say, "Let me do it." A toddler previously content to accept help now wants to do it all. Some youth ministers have fallen into the same pattern.

Here are several clues that a youth minister has unconsciously adopted the "let me do it" model of ministry.

1. The youth minister is the central figure at every event.

2. Youth workers and sponsors are given only background roles, such as driving cars or preparing refreshments.

3. Few youth join who were not personally enlisted by the youth minister.

4. The youth minister works under extreme time pressure just before a major youth event.

5. The youth program is dull during periods when the youth minister must be out of town.

Youth ministers who have adopted this model are working hard. In fact, they are working so hard that other areas of life are suffering. Their stress level runs high; they have little personal time, their health may be suffering; and they are not able to affirm significant relationships with family or friends.

Why would someone choose a model that is painful? Here are several possible explanations:

Some youth ministers feel they must justify their positions.— Youth ministers are not unique in this regard. All staff members are tempted to use busyness to justify their positions. Those who adopt this model believe they must do it all in order to convince the church that their position is worth having.

Such leaders are usually anxious for church members to know how many long hours they work. They frequently complain about how many evening and weekend hours are needed to get their work done. Unfortunately, most of these leaders have misunderstood the mind-set of the church. The church employed the youth minister to coordinate and balance all the church is doing with and for youth. The church already has shown it values that role by creating and funding the position.

Some youth ministers feel guilty delegating because they are the only ones getting paid.—This train of thought is similar to the first reason. Some youth ministers believe they must do all the work because they are on the payroll. They may believe that in delegating they are asking people to do the work for which the youth minister is getting paid.

The youth minister's unique role, coordinating the church's total ministry with youth, will easily fill one's workweek. Healthy youth ministers have found a balance between laziness and neurotically doing the work of others.

Creating opportunity for service is part of the youth minister's proper role. Delegating and enlisting others is part of true ministry. Believing that the youth minister is being paid to do everything is a mistake.

Some youth ministers feel guilty delegating because they believe they are hurting the quality of others' lives.—Most adults complain about their schedules. Youth workers, parents, and sponsors do, too. Consequently, some youth ministers believe that by enlisting adults to support ministry, they are making those adults' lives even worse. The youth ministers may just choose to do all the work themselves.

Youth ministers must be sensitive to others' time commitments. Such sensitivity includes delegating well in advance, helping leaders find creative ways to get work done, and creating a youth calendar with both youth's and adults' schedules in mind.

Giving leaders an opportunity to serve is positive not negative. Everyone is busy with something. Youth ministers can allow adults and mature youth to be busy with responsibilities that bring rewards, meaning, and purpose.

Some youth ministers are unconsciously seeking their fathers' blessings.—Unfortunately, some adults were reared by fathers who never gave them a blessing. That is, their fathers never expressed with words their affection for their children or their pride in what their children accomplished.

A mother's blessing is certainly important to children. However, the absence of the father's blessing seems to have even more psychological implications than absence of the mother's.

Youth ministers who have missed receiving their fathers' blessing enter adulthood with an emotional void. Individuals respond to that void in different ways. Some unconsciously hope their vocational performance will bring the missing blessing. They may think, "If I just work hard enough, perhaps I will measure up; and my dad will finally be proud of me."

Unfortunately, most fathers who emotionally have been unable to give a blessing in the past never change. Their children may work fruitlessly for that blessing for a lifetime. That may include years of trying to do all the work.

Youth ministers who are working so hard that they are seriously stressed and hurting key relationships need to examine carefully what is pushing them. Those who know they have missed their fathers' blessings may consider this as one factor. This insight may be a step toward a healthier approach to vocation.[1]

Some youth ministers may be workaholics.—Some youth ministers try to do all the work because they are psychologically addicted to work. They use long hours of work the same way an alcoholic uses alcohol. Long hours may be an escape from a stressful home or a way to cover over feelings of guilt or unworthiness. Working long hours may be a way to prop up a weak self-concept.

Similar to the alcoholic, the workaholic may need increasing doses to keep an equilibrium. Those with either disorder eventually are left with broken relationships and poor health.

Youth ministers seldom overcome workaholism with will power. The guidance of a professional skilled in human dynamics can be an important part of the healing process.

The Big Event Model

This model is similar to a bead necklace. The youth program is primarily a series of major events loosely strung together. Here are several clues this model is in use:

1. The youth minister uses most of his or her office time planning toward the next major event.

2. The youth budget provides large amounts for several key events and much smaller amounts for week-to-week ministry.

3. Youth newsletters, calendars, posters, and announcements spotlight big events but seldom mention weekly opportunities.

4. The youth minister spends little time equipping youth leaders for weekly ministry.

5. The youth minister is bored with conferences on effective, ongoing ministry but is attracted to materials and discussions about big events.

Youth ministers may have one of several reasons for choosing to center their programs around big events. Here are the most common:

Some youth ministers believe big events lead to consistent Christian growth.—Big events have a place in youth ministry. They add joy to life, aid outreach, and occasionally occur at a moment when a teenager is prepared to take a new step of faith. Most youth programs would be dull without them.

The key issue is balance. Events that are so large or so frequent they drain time and resources from ongoing ministry seldom lead to consistent growth. Such an approach is similar to asking teenagers to eat one big meal every three days with nothing in between. Teenagers do not grow that way physically or spiritually.

Some youth ministers grew up in a youth program built around big events.—Every church leader has a tendency to reproduce the style of ministry under which he or she grew up. Rapid changes in youth culture demand that youth ministers carefully examine those past patterns.

The divorce rate in America has doubled again just during the past ten years. Youth today are starved for caring relationships with adults. Big events seldom bond youth and leaders as do ongoing groups in the church. Most lasting growth in a teenager's life takes place in the context of relationships.

The suicide rate among youth has increased 200 percent in just the past 20 years. Many more youth today doubt life is worth living than when youth ministers were growing up. Big events seldom provide a caring environment where teenagers can share their struggles with a small group. Almost all teenagers are struggling with some personal issue they need to discuss with others. Crazy olympics, concerts, rallies, joy explosions, and two-hundred-foot banana splits all have a place; but they do not provide that setting.

Some youth ministers may have an emotional need to stay in the spotlight.—Most youth ministers want to be recognized for their work from time to time. That is appropriate.

Some youth ministers feel the need to stay in the spotlight.They realize that a succession of big events will make their work more visible and will bring them more public acclaim.

Other youth ministers put the needs of youth above their own. They find coordinating a comprehensive, balanced youth ministry to be personally rewarding. They don't need to stand in the spotlight as often to feel good about themselves or what they do.

The Pastor Model

This mode has several strengths but even more weaknesses. Here are some clues that the pastor model is operative.

1. The youth minister has led one or more of the youth organizations to give him time that was once spent in group study.

2. No quality time is provided on Wednesday evening for ongoing missions education.

3. The youth minister is responsible to the pastor while other age-group ministers are responsible to the minister of education or staff coordinator.

4. The youth minister (and possibly his or her interns) are the only leaders making an impact on school campuses.

Youth ministers who have chosen the pastor model have usually done so for positive reasons. Some have chosen this model as a reaction against an activities-only approach to youth ministry. They may know of churches that believe that "just keeping kids off the street" is all that is necessary.

Youth ministers using this model are certainly right in wanting to see spiritual growth among teens. They are also right in assuming that just a rash of activity will not necessarily lead to that growth. However, even though the goals of the pastor model are valid, the usual methods for reaching those goals are sometimes weak.

For example, a youth minister might say: "I want my young people to understand the things of God. I believe youth who hear me speak will grow. Therefore, I will ask our Youth Sunday School faculty to allow me to take most of the hour as a master teacher for youth."

The goal is admirable but educational research suggests that little long-term learning and change will occur. And when that particular youth minister leaves, strengthening a faculty that has atrophied during the pastor-model era will take years.

Also, youth ministers using the pastor model may want to ensure that nothing on the youth calendar detracts from genuine spiritual growth. Such a goal is admirable, but the implementation may be weak. In their reaction against an exclusive fun-and-games approach to youth ministry, some leaders have decided to purge from their calendars everything that appears trivial. These leaders may not realize that well-planned recreation and activities are vehicles for ministry.

For example, strengthening the body life of the youth group is New Testament ministry. Carefully structured activities provide the environment where youth learn to be open, to care, and to shape positively the lives of their peers.

Reaching new youth for Christ and church membership is also New Testament ministry. Recreation can provide an effective vehicle for reaching those youth. Matthew knew this principle when he used a fellowship meal in his home to introduce his friends to Jesus. Becoming too "spiritual" for appropriate activities may mean that spiritual goals will not be achieved.

Some youth ministers may choose the pastor model in hopes of receiving some of the positive strokes that go to a pastor. The pastors of most churches are held in high regard. Within certain bounds, that is as it should be. Youth ministers should join with other staff members and laypeople in supporting the pastor and granting him the respect his position entails.

Mature youth ministers should affirm the role of the pastor without wishing to share that unique role. Youth in a church have only one pastor. The youth minister is and should be a significant leader to youth, but he or she is not their pastor. Youth may know the youth minister better, may spend more hours with him, and may be more spiritually motivated by him; but the youth minister is not their pastor.

Some youth ministers may hope that an organizational chart and a title that identifies them with the pastor may lead to higher salaries and more esteem in the congregation. Other youth ministers believe that effectively coordinating a balanced, comprehensive ministry to and with youth will be affirmed and rewarded by the congregation.

The Balanced Youth Ministry Model

This approach to youth ministry seems to have many strengths. Here are several evidences it has been adopted.

1. The youth minister coordinates a healthy balance between special events and effective youth organizations.

2. Because of the resources and personal energy the youth minister has poured into the youth organizations, they are popular with the young people.

3. Elected youth workers report feeling they are valued partners with the youth minister.

4. The youth minister coordinates both formal and informal ways to support and educate parents of youth.

5. The youth calendar is developed by key leaders of the youth organizations, representative youth, and the youth minister.

6. Most special youth events are channeled through one or more of the youth organizations in a way that strengthens those organizations and builds deeper leader-youth relationships.

A growing number of youth ministers have chosen the balanced model approach to youth ministry. Here are several reasons this model is becoming so popular.

Some youth ministers discovered they must adopt this model or leave youth ministry.—These youth ministers began youth work by trying to do everything themselves. Because of their youthful energy and limited family responsibilities, they were able to keep up the pace for a few years.

After a while, they began to see the signs of burnout. They began to lose the joy of ministry and to feel trapped by the schedules they had created. They began to resent the fact that they carried most of the emotional load in ministry to youth.

Many of these leaders entered a time in life when spending

time with their families or closest friends became more important. The unending activities on evenings and weekends associated with the other models became a growing frustration.

These youth ministers knew that they must make some changes or leave youth ministry. Some, indeed, left their calling. Others moved toward a more balanced model of youth ministry.

Over time, they began to make other adults true partners in ministry. They began to broaden the spotlight that had been centered on them alone and to share it with the entire leadership team. They began to value the organizations and positions those leaders filled. They began to encourage relationships between youth and leaders. These youth ministers also began to channel most youth activities and special events through the ongoing youth organizations. By involving key leaders in the initial dreaming and planning stages, youth ministers found leaders eager to take a more active role in implementation.

As these new partners in ministry began to share the load, youth ministers discovered that they could get their work done in a more normal weekly schedule. Some were pleasantly surprised with the competence of lay leaders.

Youth ministers who have adopted the balanced model are able to coordinate full youth programs within a healthy number of hours each week. This opens the door to long tenures in individual churches and scores of total years in youth ministry.

Some youth ministers adopted the balanced model because they had experienced the weaknesses with one of the other models.—These youth ministers were not motivated to move toward the balanced model by a speaker or a book. They were motivated by their own frustrations with youth programs that didn't seem to make a difference.

Most youth ministers who have served 10 years or more can remember a time when their youth programs were just a blur of activities provided for youth. Many can remember literally dozens of hours spent turning the fellowship hall into a replica of a Paris cafe or summer calendars that featured something for youth almost every day.

Nothing was particularly wrong with any of the activities. They were just out of balance. After a few years of this style of programming, a number of youth ministers began to watch the lives of their high-school graduates. Some leaders had to wonder whether six years of busyness had genuinely prepared these young adults to live responsible, godly lives.

Some youth ministers began to say: "Yes, I got lots of compliments with the Paris cafe I created for the banquet. But what if I had involved leaders and youth and had planned simpler decorations? I then would have had 10 more hours to give to strengthening our Youth Sunday School or counseling troubled parents. I know which would have made more difference."

Some youth ministers have moved toward the balanced model because they believe it is more biblical.—These youth ministers believe the call to be a minister is primarily a call to be an equipper of the saints. In youth ministry this means their primary call is to equip youth parents, youth workers, and even mature youth to do the work of youth ministry.

In a sense these parents, workers, and mature youth are the ministers to youth. The staff member is the coordinator and equipper of youth ministers.

This view of ministry is consistent with Ephesians 4:11-13. Many would view the position of the contemporary youth minister as implied in verse 11. Verse 12 then explains what the youth minister's role is. Several translations of Scripture clarify that role: "To fit his People for the work of the ministry."[2] "To equip God's people for work in his service."[3] "His gifts were made that Christians might be properly equipped for their service."[4]

One youth minister can no longer manage all the logistics of youth programming. One youth minister cannot find the hours that quality time with every youth on roll needs and deserves. One youth minister cannot win and reach all the lost youth in a community. And one youth minister certainly cannot respond to all the personal and family crises that now arise in youth culture. The equipping ministry inherent in the balanced model is absolutely essential.

Some youth ministers have chosen the balanced model because they believe Christian growth is itself balanced.—Neither the "let me do it," big event, nor pastor model of youth ministry places much emphasis on the ongoing youth organizations.

This almost always means youth ministers using one of these models are leading a ministry that is spiritually unbalanced.

The youth organizations have been specifically designed to speak to each area of Christian growth. Youth Sunday School teaches youth the biblical revelation. Leaders guide youth to discover timeless truths of Scripture and to make direct application of those truths to their lives. Youth Sunday School also challenges youth and leaders to win teenagers to Christ and to reach them for church membership.

Youth Discipleship Training enables youth to grow in their personal walks with God. Youth encounter issues such as ethical decision making, Baptist doctrine, Baptist history, and church polity and organization. In addition, youth learn the biblical background and the skills they need to do personal Bible study, to pray meaningfully, to memorize Scripture, and to share their faith. They also receive valuable training in church leadership roles.

Acteens, Pioneer Royal Ambassadors, and High School Baptist Young Men give youth a heart for missions. These organizations guide youth to discover truths about missions in Scripture, the way the church has spread the gospel down through history, and what Southern Baptists are doing to win the world today. Youth discover practical ways to support this missions enterprise through prayer and giving and to become directly involved in ministry through mission action and personal witnessing.

Youth music enables youth to be good stewards of the gifts God has given them. Music training and participation deepen young peoples' understanding of and growth from worship experiences. Music gives youth unique opportunities to share their faith within and outside the walls of the church. Music provides youth a way to express their personal praise to God and a way to remember biblical truths.

Youth who participate in youth music, a missions organization, Youth Discipleship Training, and Youth Sunday School each week have a significant advantage. They receive the experiences that make balanced Christian growth possible.

Keeping each of these organizations effective and appealing to youth is hard work. Enlisting, training, and motivating leaders, providing materials, supporting out-of-class projects, and doing promotion take time. Youth ministers using the balanced model believe this is essential time if balanced Christian growth is to occur.

Balanced-model youth ministers use recreation as a ministry vehicle. They coordinate creative recreation for youth, parents, and workers as a way to accomplish youth ministry goals.

Most recreation plans are designed to support the work of the youth organizations. Many of those plans flow out of experiences youth and leaders have had in class, or they are designed to enrich relationships for future learning experiences. Quality, balanced recreation can strengthen evangelism and outreach, reveal God-given talents, add joy to life, strengthen families, and promote the stewardship of one's own body.

Youth ministers who have adopted the balanced model balance the time they give to youth, workers, and parents. Their equipping and supporting ministry with the adults who serve in the youth organizations receives about one third of their time. Combination staff members give one third of that part of the week they are able to commit to youth ministry.

Well-balanced youth ministers also give about a third of the time available to teenagers. This includes the time they spend directly with young people and the time they spend preparing to be with them. The hours youth ministers spend directly with youth give them opportunities to affirm, encourage, counsel, inspire, confront, and unconditionally love youth.

Youth ministers employing the balanced model also commit a third of the time available to the parents of youth. This includes time they spend in conversation, counseling, planning, and leading or coordinating parenting events.

Youth ministry calendars developed with the balanced model usually contain events such as parent support groups, parent education seminars, parent and youth dialogues, parent and youth retreats, and parent and youth mission experiences.[5]

Youth ministers modeling this approach to ministry believe a balance between the positive influence of the home and the church provides the greatest impact on youth. Youth ministers using other models may miss this strength.

The ultimate aim of a balanced youth ministry is to win lost youth to Christ. Each youth organization prepares youth to share their faith. When youth ministers strengthen those organizations, they strengthen evangelism. Youth leaders are in ideal positions to win youth to Christ. Youth ministers who equip youth leaders strengthen evangelism. Families influence youth toward or away from Christ. Youth ministers who expand their ministry to families strengthen evangelism. Each of these ministries compliments youth ministers' commitment to share personally their faith with youth.

The "let me do it," big event, and pastor models of youth ministry each have some strengths but even more weaknesses. The balanced model of Southern Baptist youth ministry offers the best opportunity for long-term effectiveness.

---

[1]The Sunday School Board offers an excellent week-long experience for staff members interested in exploring how personal issues may be affecting their work. Call (615) 251-2052 for more information about professional and career development seminars.

[2]From *The Twentieth Century New Testament: A Translation into Modern English* (New York: Fleming H. Revell, 1904).

[3]From *The New English Bible.* Copyright © The Delegates of the Oxford University Press and the Syndics of the Cambridge University Press, 1961, 1970. Reprinted by permission.

[4]Reprinted with permission MacMillan Publishing Co., Inc. from J. B. Phillips: *The New Testament in Modern English*, Revised Edition. © J. B. Phillips 1958, 1960, 1972.

[5]For more information on coordinating events for parents and youth families, see Richard Ross and G. Wade Rowatt, Jr., *Ministry with Youth and Their Parents* (Nashville: Convention Press, 1986).

PERSONAL LEARNING ACTIVITIES

1. Name and describe three models for doing youth ministry.

2. Why do some youth ministers follow the "let me do it" model?

3. Why do some youth ministers choose the big event model?

4. What are the indications that a youth minister has chosen the pastor model?

5. Name several advantages of using the balanced model.

CHAPTER 5

THE MINISTER OF YOUTH'S WORK WITH YOUTH

Your Relationship with Youth

Love

Youth today are no different from youth of other generations in their need for love and discipline! They struggle with emotions—feelings of rejection, fear, and hurts that many times they do not share with anyone.

Many youth ministers struggle with their role with youth. They try to be friends so much that they disregard the loving but firm relationship that can exist between youth and a youth minister. Youth ministers need to get to know youth's hurts and fears so that they will understand them. Youth ministers also must learn to treat youth not as peers but as individuals who need and deserve ministry and care. Youth must know their youth minister not just as friend but as minister first and then friend.

J. B. Collingsworth
Adult/youth
consultant
Louisiana Baptist
Convention
Alexandria, Louisiana

Consistency is a key word in relating to youth. Young people need to know that in a crazy, mixed-up world an adult who is a nonparent really does care. The youth minister must always care for youth even when they are unlovable. Sometimes youth will vent their feelings and frustrations toward the youth minister no matter how hard you try to care. Many times they will test you to see if you really do mean what you say about unconditional love or if you love them only when it is convenient and easy.

An important part of the youth-minister relationship is caring enough to confront. When a youth is engaged in unhealthy behaviors such as sexual activity, drinking, or illicit drugs, someone needs to say: "I am concerned. I know you have a problem." You do not have to be specific about the problem; allow them to open up to you. Do not condemn but genuinely show concern. You must have a relationship with a young person before such a confrontation. Youth must know that you have their best interests at heart, or bitter feelings can develop. Parents often want a youth minister to solve all their teenager's problems. This is an impossible task and should not be tackled!

Jesus spent much of His three-year ministry reaching out to those the world considered to be unlovely. If we model the kind of love Jesus had for others, we must be willing to go to all people in all places. Caring for popular, attractive young people in the group is easy. But youth ministers must also demonstrate love for the unpopular, the unattractive, the unchurched, the unsaved, and those who do not always support the youth minister. All youth are valuable in God's sight.

A young man in a church I served several years ago had a difficult time fitting in with the rest of the youth group. He was often withdrawn and stayed apart from the group. Today he is a strong Christian minister with a bright and positive future. God changed his life. Many adults loved and encouraged him, and he worked hard to grow. God transformed him.

Affirmation

Youth need lots of encouragement. Our society does not offer much encouragement to anyone. Find ways to emphasize the positive. Be willing to touch, to put your arm around them.

One way to encourage youth is to write notes to them. Another is to affirm youth with birthday cards. One friend has his youth birthdays on his computer. He sends prebirthday notes at three, six, and nine months prior to the big day. This way he is certain to touch all of his young people several times per year with a note and a kind word.

The youth minister can have a ready file of letters. These can include:

• An encouragement letter to students who accept Christ and need to be baptized.

• Letters of appreciation for work done or involvement in some special project.

• Letters to youth who give their lives to church-related vocational ministry.

• Letters to those who experience a death in their family.

• Letters to students who visit your church. Having several different letters on file would help prevent visitors' receiving the same letter over and over again.

• Letters that say "I care" can be comforting to students involved in their own personal struggles and crises. If you have access to a computer, you can have form letters in memory that can be quickly modified for each use.

Verbally let youth know that you appreciate them. Compliment them on those posters they did, the clothes that look good on them, and the phone calls they made. When they achieve in sports or become a cheerleader, tell them you are proud of them.

Encourage youth workers to help keep you informed of these significant events. The entire adult leadership team can cut clippings from the newspaper and place these on the youth bulletin board.

Discipline

Youth today are crying out for discipline. They want boundaries and guidelines. When parents discipline a child, that child becomes free to enjoy life in ways that would be impossible without discipline. Youth respond to rules if they perceive that you have their best interest at heart.

How can you do this?

1. Start out with a firm and loving stand. Becoming more lenient is easy, but becoming stricter after you have been lax is difficult.

2. State rules for events and enforce them. If a youth violates the rules, do what you said you would do.

3. Inform all sponsors for events about their roles and how to discipline.

4. Write out guidelines for adults, especially for overnight events. Sharing responsibility for discipline will keep you from having to be the heavy all the time. When a big problem arises, send the youth home with instruction to tell his/her parents what happened. Check with his parents to find out if they were informed. If they were not, sit down with them, tell them what happened, and discuss alternative helps. Be prepared to minister to the entire family if needed.

Your Insights into Youth

Characteristics

Youth are on a roller-coaster ride every day with their feelings. Everything that happens is big to them. Their personalities are changing, and their hormones are playing dirty tricks on them. Haim Ginott described adolescence as a "period of curative madness, in which every teenager has to remake his personality."[1]

Their number one focus is on themselves, and the question they are asking is "Who am I?" Their constant concerns range from "How do I look?" to "Who cares?" Paul Irwin in *The Care and Counseling of Youth in the Church* stated that adolescents have four crucial needs: (1) finding acceptance within community, (2) deepening interpersonal communication, (3) shaping an ideology or vision of life, (4) achieving vocational direction.[2] They need affirmation about who they are. They are real persons now not persons on the way to becoming real persons.

To give youth the kind of ministry they need, you also need to be aware of the developmental guidelines for junior-high and senior-high youth. They are in constant transition. They are probably thinking about dating, becoming interested in the opposite sex, moody, cliquish, asking to be independent of parental authority, worrying about the way they dress, and easily influenced by friends. All of this begins as they enter adolescence. David Self listed some developmental characteristics for ages 12 to 17 in his book *Reaching Youth Through the Sunday School*.

12
- Energetic and enthusiastic.
- Increasingly socially conscious, wanting to belong to a group.
- Open to bring their friends to Sunday School and to other worthwhile activities.
- Not comfortable in one-on-one witnessing encounters; prefer group witnessing encounters.
- Seldom ready for deep, abstract questions on salvation; concerned instead with God's love, their sin, and their personal relationship to Christ.

13-14
- Enthusiastic, but inhibitions are appearing.
- Sometimes moody.
- Developing a sense of purpose in their lives.
- Deepening their sense of responsibility for fellow youth.
- Becoming dependent on friends as a support group.

15-16
- Experiencing many outside influences on their lives—cars, dates, jobs, etc.
- Increasingly mobile and independent
- Now sometimes having an option of attending church.
- More interested in the opposite sex.
- More comfortable in one-on-one situations.
- Increasingly able to think in abstract terms and to understand deeper theological issues.

17
- More capable of leadership with other younger youth.
- Role model for younger youth.

• More interested in participating if challenged to lead, perform, create, etc.

• Facing many outside pressures and decisions which might make them especially open to the gospel.[3]

Sometimes it is easy to forget what it was like to be a teenager. Referring to this list or reading other sources about youth's age characteristics from time to time may be helpful.

Values

"A value is something that has worth and is desirable."[4] One task of youth ministers is to help youth learn to value themselves. They must feel good about who they are before they are able to value other people, beliefs, and principles. How we see ourselves strongly affects how we reach others.

I always encourage youth with low self-esteem to look in the mirror every day and say: "Hi, _____! (their name) I like you! You're OK!" I tell them to do this until they can honestly mean it. Once they begin to mean it, they are able to perceive other things as valuable.

Values help us to perceive life. Some people value and hold high beliefs that others consider to be unimportant. Another task of youth ministers is to help youth learn what is important.

Young people place so much emphasis on cheerleading, playing sports, being in the band, and other activities. All of these are good. But if these things are valued higher than one's relationship with Christ, then values need readjustment.

Culture affects values. Some friends from two different cultures recently divorced. Many of their problems stemmed from their opposite views and values which were shaped by their different backgrounds and cultures. What was acceptable to one was not to the other. They did not share common values when they married, and this eventually led to their split. Youth need to know their values before marriage! We must get them to identify their values and encourage them to keep high standards and ideals. We need to help youth determine what they prize the most.

Values do change. They should become more concrete as we

mature. Ask youth to name their purpose in life, to set goals, and to determine in light of gifts and talents what vocation they should enter. Help them to see beyond today and know that the choices they make will truly affect their system of values. They need to see that they must develop their own set of values in order to become the person God wants them to be.

Positive Peer Influence

A strong youth group is almost a Christian subculture in itself. Is this wrong? Surely not. If a youth group excludes unsaved youth, it is. If, on the other hand, everyone feels included and loved, you can really do some exciting things.

How does this happen? You must begin to teach young people how to invite their friends to be a part of your youth group. As youth see that new youth can come, feel accepted, and have a good time, other youth will want to bring their friends.

You may need to plan activities and programs to teach youth how to build friendships. Use role playing to help them understand how new youth feel when they come to church for the first time. Talk to them about how to respond to someone else's uniqueness.

Have you ever met a youth who did not want to be where the action is? As youth get excited about their youth group, they will want to spread the good news to all their friends. They begin to exert positive peer influence over their friends. Going to church is exciting when a young person is right with God. As youth exert this positive peer influence, more youth will be reached; and the youth group will grow.

Your youth ministry can be the most exciting and imaginative group for youth in your area if you dream big enough dreams. Youth's lives will be changed. Some youth may begin to attend church because it is the social place to be; but you then have the opportunity to shape youth lives, to lead them to Christ, and to help them grow as disciples.

Your Work with Youth

Evangelism

Youth ministers must be about the business of reaching others and showing young people how they can reach others, too. If we have a fervent zeal to see people saved, we will impart that to every youth worker and young person in our youth group. Leaving evangelism to the youth evangelist who comes in for the next revival will soon lessen your personal effectiveness.

A youth minister's first priority should be to see youth saved and to see them grow as disciples. Seeing youth saved and growing as believers will bring vitality and excitement to your church. But evangelism, like any other worthwhile objective, requires planning. The youth minister must plan for evangelism. This planning may include a specific method for reaching people such as WOW or CWT.[5] But planning for evangelism should permeate all planning for youth events.[6]

You can get started by taking one or two youth visiting with you. Allow them to see you sharing a verbal witness. Ask one of them to share a personal testimony during the visit. If a youth accepts Christ, have one of the visiting team members tell your whole group about it at your next event.

Then be prepared! Be sure your Sunday School is prepared for growth—that workers and youth are receptive to new people and include them with excitement and that physical space also encourages growth.

Get youth workers excited and challenged to become soul-winners. Have them commit to visit and take youth with them. Keep your prospect file up-to-date. Survey youth to find out who the new people are in their schools. Have youth complete a registration card at every event.

The following ideas may stimulate your thinking to other ways your group can reach new youth for Christ:

● Print school football/basketball schedules on cards with the plan of salvation on the back.

● Sponsor a day of handing out tracts or putting them in lockers at school.

● Print book covers with the plan of salvation on the back.

● Sponsor fifth-quarter events (fellowships after home football games) and encourage church youth to bring their friends.

● Present the gospel at home Bible studies and give youth opportunity to respond.

Youth may be saved almost anywhere; but they need someone to tell them.

Ministry by Youth

Youth need to be involved in service opportunities and mission endeavors to grasp the importance of living out their faith. They will develop and grow from these opportunities.

Reflect on your own experiences. Remember the youth who went on a mission trip, caught a vision of a world in need, then came back to live for Christ, and perhaps surrendered for church-related vocational ministry. Or what about the uninvolved youth who first got involved because he could make posters and was asked to help with a big youth event. Remember those? All youth need to be challenged by participating in missions and ministry opportunities. They will grow and learn from these wonderful experiences.

Meet with caring youth workers and youth to plan missions and ministry events that will help youth garner self-esteem as they meet genuine needs. The church should take the lead in opening doors of service to youth. Youth can minister through revival teams, in puppet and clown groups, as canvassers and more! Churches should both do things for youth and give them opportunities to do for themselves and others. A youth ministry should equip youth to minister.

Pastoral Care/Counseling

Youth today live in an age of stress. To minister to these youth, youth ministers need to have more than surface contact with those in their youth groups. Youth ministers need to know individual youth well enough to know their needs. To know youth this well means first to let'youth know we care. Caring may mean going to football games to watch them play, calling the girl who didn't make the cheerleading squad, dropping by a home where the parents are getting a divorce. Whatever the need, we must be sensitive to the Holy Spirit and ask for His guidance to help us minister to youth where they are.

Joe White, in *Looking for Leadership*, offered help in counseling youth. He suggested asking youth who come for help three simple questions. Let them know that you are going to ask these three questions and tell that each time you ask a question they must give a different answer. The goal in this process is help youth work toward solving a problem themselves.

The questions are: (1) What's wrong? or, What do you want? (2) How are you feeling? (3) What are you doing about the problem? These really work! Listen to what they say. Lovingly ask these same questions over and over. After a few minutes, and at the right time, say, "What do you need to do to change the situation or solve the problem"? Ask if they are willing to do what they have suggested and if life will be different if they do.

Before asking the questions, consider what you must do to make this plan work well. First, you must show empathy with the student through your expressions and your eyes and with your words. Youth need to know by your actions, both verbal and nonverbal, that you understand and care. You should also be slow to jump to conclusions and offer premature advice. Many times youth will tell you the surface problem without getting to the real problem.[7]

To really touch the lives of youth, we must do the following:

Be respectful.—Respect who they are. Encourage them to open up but honor their privacy.

Be honest.—When asked your opinion, tell them. Encourage them to be honest by being honest yourself. Point out areas where they can improve.

Be forgiving.—When youth disappoint you, always be willing to forgive and to go the second mile.

Be loving.—In each relationship, show youth they are loved. In whatever relationship, remember Jesus' admonition in John 13:34-35, "A new commandment I give unto you, . . . that ye also love one another. By this shall all men [young people] know that ye are my disciples, if ye have love one to another."

Crisis Intervention

Attempts at suicide, sex before marriage, the breakup of homes, child abuse, affluence or the lack of it, and drug and alcohol abuse are some of the crises youth face. Because of the severity of these problems, you may be called frequently for counseling or crisis intervention. You may not have all the answers; but if you exhibit unconditional love and concern for the entire family, you will have begun to minister effectively.

Your job may be to refer. Keep a file of Christian counselors, drug and alcohol rehabilitation centers, hospitals, and family services. Be aware of social service agencies and what they offer. Do not try to tackle problems too big for you. If you need to share something told to you in confidence, be sure to have permission to share that information.

Through the years, youth have come to me to share guilt over abortions, teenage pregnancies, drug abuse, physical abuse, and other crises. I have always tried to refrain from the "open-jaw effect." Be able to take the shock. Accept youth as they are, and do not condemn them. You may condemn what they do, but do not condemn them.

Many youth ministers have seen the need for and have begun a crisis counseling program. Some youth ministers have made their availability for counseling known by using a youth hotline. The recorded message details youth events for the week followed by a number to call if they have a problem and need to talk to someone. Parents can call also for youth information or for counseling.

Before beginning this ministry, adults who are willing to have their telephone number placed on the hotline need to be trained.Invite a competent, qualified counselor to train youth parents and youth workers who want to be involved and who would be telephone listeners. Train them to refer when necessary.

A different person should be on call each day. Persons who volunteer need to be aware of the commitment needed and the demands this ministry will make on already busy schedules. But this ministry can be rewarding for all involved.[8]

Helping Youth Find God's Will

"Finding God's will" may sound as if God is hiding it from us. Terminology can be evasive. We must use the right terminology in working with youth who want to determine God's best for their lives. We need to explain that God's will is not hidden.

Many people do not attach a lot of dignity to their vocations. They get up and go to work every day but have no idea why they do what they do except to bring home a paycheck. Encourage young people to seek all avenues of interest. Provide opportunities for them to meet adults in various occupations and to ask them questions about their careers.

Help youth to gain a positive self-image. An accurate self-understanding will help youth make the right career choice. We also need to teach youth to understand and discover their spiritual gifts and pray with them as they ask God to show them His perfect will for their lives. "Young people need encouragement in discovering their talents and abilities. Reassure them that God's vocational will is practical. It is to be found among the things that need to be done, among the things they can do well, and among the things they enjoy doing."[9]

Creating Loyalty

In a day when loyalties are not often taught, we must help students to learn what loyalty is. They do not need blind allegiance to a person or a cause, but they do need to discern the important things in life to which they need to give attention and allegiance.

One's loyalty ought to be to the church. If parents fail to teach this, the youth minister may be able to fill the gap and do so. Youth ministers need to exhibit such a love for Christ's church that youth grasp its importance. As they see you making church an important part of your life, they will begin to understand that the church is more than just a building and a group of people. They will want to be there to worship and to grow.

The most important loyalty is to Christ. Many youth ministers create a great following, but they need to communicate to youth the message, "Follow Jesus, not me." Youth cannot, in reality, see or touch Jesus; they can, however, see and touch you. Youth ministers must be examples and direct youth to focus on God.

As they develop their allegiance toward Him, you sit on the sidelines and encourage them to strive continually to be more like Him.

Ministry to youth is rewarding and challenging. Allow youth to express themselves and present their ideas. Gear your ministry to meet them at their points of need. Teach them to follow Christ and His commands that they too will be ministers.

---

[1] Haim G. Ginott, *Between Parent and Teenager* (New York: Macmillan, 1969), 25.

[2] Paul B. Irwin, *The Care and Counseling of Youth in the Church* (Philadelphia: Fortress Press, 1975), 17.

[3] David Self, *Reaching Youth Through the Sunday School* (Nashville: Convention Press, 1979), 48-51.

[4] Carl A. Elder, *Youth and Values: Getting Self Together* (Nashville: Broadman Press, 1978), 21.

[5] For more information on WOW (Win Our World) or CWT (Continuing Witness Training), write the Home Mission Board, 1350 Spring Street, NW, Atlanta, Georgia 30367.

[6] For more information on planning for evangelism, see Richard Ross, comp., *Youth Ministry Planbook 4* (Nashville: Convention Press, 1989).

[7] Joe White, *Looking for Leadership* (Branson, MO: Operation Challenge, 1984), 49-51.

[8] For more information on crisis ministry, see Richard Ross and Judi Hayes, comp., *Ministry with Youth in Crisis* (Nashville: Convention Press, 1988).

[9] Richard D. Dobbins, *Venturing into a Teenager's World* (Old Tappan, NJ: Fleming H. Revell, 1986), 125.

PERSONAL LEARNING ACTIVITIES

1. Describe several specific ways a youth minister can describe youth.

2. Give several steps to ensuring discipline at youth events.

3. How can a youth minister encourage evangelism in the youth group?

4. How can a church begin to get youth involved in missions or ministry?

5. What is the youth minister's role in creating loyalty among youth?

CHAPTER 6

THE MINISTER OF YOUTH'S WORK WITH ADULT LEADERS

Serving in a ministry that helps to shape young lives is a privilege and a challenge. Those who work with teenagers have as their goal to ensure that youth are guided to grow in a positive and Christlike manner.

You can choose one of two basic ways to build a youth ministry in your church. The first approach I would describe as the lone-ranger approach. In the old TV western, each episode of "The Lone Ranger" had basically the same plot. The bad guys were defeating the good guys. In each incident at just the right moment, the Lone Ranger would ride in on his white horse, Silver, and save the day.

With his trusty sidekick, Tonto, the Lone Ranger could handle any and every situation that existed. Nothing was so large or complicated that he could not ride in and save the day.

Chris Liebrum
Sunday School
associate
The Baptist General
Convention of Texas
Dallas, Texas

Of course, the story of the Lone Ranger is a bit unrealistic. Equally unrealistic is thinking that youth ministry can be handled with the same philosophy. No youth minister alive has the physical, mental, or spiritual ability to ride in on a white horse and handle each and every situation.

If "The Lone Ranger" was before your time, you probably are more familiar with the recent series, "Hillstreet Blues." Basically the plots were the same as in "The Lone Ranger." The bad guys took advantage of the good guys. And most of the time by the end of each show, the good guys won. At this point, however, the similarities end. If you ever watched "Hillstreet Blues," you know that it was a study in teamwork. Any given episode included several people—a street cop working on the case, a detective helping to investigate it, and the chief always informed and ready to help in any way he could. Also involved were people working at the front desk of the station and a number of other characters who did their job well so that the precinct ran smoothly. In short, the show modeled a team effort.

If youth ministry in your church enjoys long-term success, members will join together in a team effort. All members will do their assigned tasks, but everyone will work together for a common purpose.

To build an effective youth ministry, you must build the team around you to help facilitate the task. As youth minister, you assume the role of chief or captain of this team. Together you and other adult workers with youth can reach teenagers for Christ.

This chapter offers suggestions in four basic areas to help you work with adults in your youth ministry. These areas are enlistment, training, motivation and support, and personal ministry.

Enlistment

Enlistment of adult leaders is the cornerstone, the foundation, for building a good youth ministry. Proper and quality enlistment can circumvent many problems down the road.

Begin the process by praying about your needs. Ask for God's help and guidance in the selection process.

Each adult who works with youth is vitally important. Choose the best persons possible to fill youth leadership positions. Never allow a time crunch or job vacancy to force you into just finding anyone to fill a slot. Having an open job in a youth leadership position may be frustrating, but having the wrong person in the job all year may be even more of a problem if the worker is not committed to youth or to the task at hand.

Finding Youth Workers

Finding faithful youth workers may be difficult, especially when you are new in a church. A few suggestions may help you find those loyal workers.

A good barometer for commitment is attendance at midweek services. Those who faithfully attend church on Wednesday night show that their church has a high propriety in their weekly schedule. Another reason to check out the Wednesday night crowd is that many youth ministry projects and organizations will meet on Wednesday night. For a number of churches Wednesday night is the time for Sunday School weekly workers meeting, Acteens, RAs, and others. Many youth ministries have a strong Wednesday night youth prayer meeting or worship event. Youth leaders are also strong role models for youth, so seeing their leaders at church on Wednesday, knowing they are present and available, is important to youth.

When you're looking for quality youth leaders, don't overlook new members. After each worship service introduce yourself to people who have just joined your church. Talk with them briefly about the church's youth ministry, and watch for other opportunities to build on your initial conversation. Some new members will quickly share with you their past experience as youth workers in their previous church. Before enlisting a new member of your church to work in youth ministry, a phone call to their previous pastor or youth minister could be helpful.

Try to be attentive to your role as an adult member of the church. Look for opportunities to get to know other adults. Regularly attend social functions of the adult Sunday School departments, for example. Through informal visitation over coffee and donuts you may find some of those quality youth workers who are sitting in an adult Sunday School class every week.

Encouraging persons with strong leadership potential to attend a prospective youth worker training session could be a great help in your enlistment. Some people who might be reluctant to volunteer to work in youth ministry could be excited after attending a multiweek training session designed just for them. Thisprospective youth worker training session might include an overview of the youth ministry in your church and a discussion of the adolescent changes that teenagers experience. A total interpretation on the philosophy of your youth ministry and an overview of all the program organizations in your youth ministry would be valuable information to new workers.

At the conclusion of your training time, some might want to specialize in a specific program area such as Sunday School, Discipleship Training, missions education, or music.

Including Adults from Various Groups

Potential youth workers may be college students, parents of singles, or senior adults. Don't overlook any of these groups when enlisting youth leaders, but consider strengths and weaknesses of these age groups and of individuals in each group.

College students can be a great source for leadership and youth ministry. They possess three characteristics essential in being a good youth worker—time, energy, and enthusiasm. Look for mature leaders among your college students. As the former youth minister for many of your college students, you will be aware of the capabilities of these students. College students make excellent workers with the junior-high students. Younger youth enjoy the vitality of college-age leaders, and they are more willing to have them as leaders than older youth who may be close to the age of the college student.

Parents of youth are also a tremendous resource inthe area of youth leadership. They have a vested interest in the success of your youth ministry. They see their involvement in youth ministry not only as a help to their Lord and church but also to their own children. Youth parents should talk with their teenagers about the possibilities of their involvement in the youth program. To some teenagers the idea of their parents being in volved in such activities as fellowships, Bible study, retreats is exciting. To other teenagers having their parents around would be devastating. Either way, a family discussion would allow everyone to express an opinion and to feel that all were considered in the decision-making process.

Single adults can also be of great service to a youth ministry. Their schedule may allow them more time to give for youth activities, and many singles may find relating to youth personally fulfilling.

Don't automatically assume that senior adults are just too old to work with teenagers. In many situations this is not the case. Many senior adults are retired and have more time to give to youth ministry. This time could be used in outreach and visitation. Their time can be used in ongoing ministry projects such as crisis ministry with teenagers, programs for unwed teenage mothers, a suicide hotline, and in many other fulfilling ways.

Preparing for Excuses

As you approach people to invite them to be a part of the church's youth ministry leadership team, some excuses for not working seem to come up repeatedly. Being aware of these reasons for not working may help you be prepared to deal with them. Here are a few of the most commonly heard excuses.

Lack of time.—This certainly is a fundamental consideration in working with young people. Our society seems to move faster and faster every day, and time seems to slip away. The American family has demands that were not present generations ago. Husbands and fathers are working one and sometimes two jobs to make ends meet. Wives and mothers are also working outside the home in an increasingńumber just to supply the basic essentials for the family. Free time has become a precious commodity. As a youth minister, you must be prepared to give realistic time expectations to potential workers. Some adults may not have enough time to work in your youth ministry, but an accurate assessment of the time required will help them to make that decision intelligently.

Fear of working with teenagers.—Some grown men in your church would rather face a raging bull than teach a seventh-grade boys Sunday School class. The fear is not of the teenagers themselves; it is mainly fear of the unknown. A good response to this fear is to invite potential leaders to attend or chaperone a retreat, a youth fellowship, a Sunday School class, or a youth camp. After being around teenagers for a while, they will soon understand that teenagers are real people, too.

Lack of training to teach teenagers.—This legitimate reason for not working with youth can be countered by having in place an ongoing trainingprogram to inform and equip potential adults to work in youth ministry much like the one discussed earlier in this chapter.

Lack of confidence.—The potential worker who says, "I am not sharp enough to work with teenagers," needs more confidence. Some adults have the misconception that in order to work with teenagers an adult must be sharp, witty, and funny. You must communicate to adults that they will be successful in youth ministry only when they come across to teenagers as being genuine. If God has given you the ability to be witty, then be witty around teenagers. If your personality tends to be laid back, then be laid back around teenagers. The important thing is to be who you are. Teenagers have a unique ability to identify someone who is being a fraud, not genuine. As adults of different personality types work with youth, they will find that youth also have different personality types. Each personality type will appeal to a segmentóf teenagers.

Working with the Nominating Committee

Theńominating committee for years has been responsible for finding and enlisting leaders for the church. This group can also be a great help in locating or evaluating potential youth workers. Cooperate with them, and they will often give you names of excellent youth workers you may not know.

The youth minister should be seen as a resource person to the committee. In an orderly and professional way, the youth minister may submit to the nominating committee suggestions for committee members, Sunday School department directors and teachers, Discipleship Training leaders, RA and High School Baptist Young Men directors, and Acteens leaders.

Working relationships are important in any organization, and it is certainly important in youth ministry. Workers tend to feel responsible to the person who enlisted them. So youth ministers should enlist heads of program organizations, the Youth Sunday School division director, for example. At that point the division director would enlist department directors, and department directors would enlist teachers, workers, and outreach leaders.

This process does not exclude the youth minister from helping in enlistment. For example, you have observed a person in your church who would be an excellent junior-high girls teacher. You might approach that person and ask about her interest in teaching eighth-grade girls. You might say something similar to this: "Mary, I think you would make an excellent eighth-grade girls Sunday School teacher. I am going to contact Bob Williams, the junior-high department director, and suggest that he talk with you about teaching in that department."

By handling enlistment this way, you have made the contact; but you are also including the department director. Enlisting through proper channels encourages laypeople in your youth ministry to act as the responsible leaders they are.

Training

Training About Youth

One of the best ways to build a great youth ministry is to build a team of volunteers to help you do the work of youth ministry. The first step to building this team is to enlist people. Following close behind enlistment must be training. No one in the business world would ever consider thrusting people into a new situation without first equipping that individual to do the task. In the same way the adults enlisted to help in youth ministry must be properly equipped to do their jobs.

Most adults would benefit from a periodic review of the characteristics of teenagers and a knowledge of the world of teenagers today. A basic and simple survey of adolescent development could go a long way in helping laypeople to understand teenagers.

Teenagers are distinct in many of their actions and characteristics. Many of their mood swings and bizarre behavior can directly be related to mental and physical changes that occur during the adolescent years. A trained adult will likely be more patient and understanding of a teenager's actions.

Several good resources are available for training in the area of adolescent development. One of the best is Daniel Aleshire's *Understanding Today's Youth*.[1] *Living with Teenagers* and *equipping youth* are good ongoing periodicals from the Baptist Sunday School Board that can give you information from time to time about teenage development. A simple but clear understanding of the teenage years can be a great foundation for adults who will work in your youth ministry.

The teenagers of the 1990s live in a different world from that experienced by most of the adults in their youth. In the last decade chemical abuse, suicide, premarital sex, and family break-ups are just a few of the problems teenagers face every day. Adults working with teenagers need to have a clear picture of this teenage world. Include training for adults that informs them about the nature of the youth community around them and gives them information about specific temptations and crises your youth face every day. This kind of training needs to be more than just a one-time event. An ongoing update is needed.

As a youth minister, you are a professional in the area of youth work. Your leadership team has a right to expect you to be aware of issues and trends in youth concerns. One good resource is your local newspaper. Read and clip articles that relate to the youth trends in your community. Your local newspaper, in most cases, will serve as a barometer of the moral climate in your area.

A good book in this area is Merton Strommen's *Five Cries of Youth*.[2] The book *Ministry with Youth in Crisis* and the new tape series *The 24-Hour Counselor* are also helpful resources.[3] Although specifically designed for youth in crisis, the tapes can give adults an intimate picture of the questions teenagers are asking.

Training About Their Jobs

Adult workers also need training in the specific program area in which they will be working. Many adult leaders will be working in Youth Sunday School as division directors, department directors, teachers, outreach leaders, or secretaries. Some may help staff your Discipleship Training program; while others will give leadership in the mission education organizations with RAs, High School Baptist Young Men, and Acteens.

A starting point for training is job expectation. Adult workers should clearly understand what you expect of them in their tasks. You may communicate with them directly, but giving them something to read and reread will also be helpful. Most of the jobs for youth program organizations have printed job descriptions. Many of these are available through your state convention offices. The program organizations have books and provide training events that will help you train your people.

Training Opportunities

Who provides all this training? Does the youth minister need to do all the training? Does the youth minister need to go with groups of youth workers to Glorieta or Ridgecrest each summer?

Southern Baptists are fortunate in having a full range of training opportunities available. Ridgecrest and Glorieta are certainly options. All church program organizations conduct training weeks each summer. These weeklong experiences will develop qualified leaders and build team spirit as workers share fellowship and travel experiences. Of course, going to a week at Ridgecrest or Glorieta for each area of youth ministry is impractical; but you might choose one week each summer over a five-year period. You can contact Glorieta or Ridgecrest or the Conference Center Section of the Baptist Sunday School Board for dates.

Your state convention provides training experiences for you that might be more accessible. These varied training events occur throughout the year. Contact the appropriate leader in your state office or watch your state paper for information about upcoming events.

Your local association of Southern Baptist churches provides for you yet another avenue of training experiences. These

events are planned specifically to meet your needs and are likely most convenient for you and your youth leaders. These events are usually one- or two-night events, and in most cases transportation is not a problem and lodging is not needed.
Convention, state, and associational training events are good tools for training your adult workers. Some of these denominational events will have a small charge to cover expenses; many will have no charge at all. Lodging, food, and transportation expenses will vary based on location and circumstance.

In addition to all the denomination has to offer in training youth workers is the training you provide in your church. You may be the best trainer of your leadership team. You obviously know the specific needs of your team and can custom design your training to meet the direct needs of your people. You also have control of the date for training opportunities in your own church. Books available through Baptist Book Stores will help you with your local training efforts. Many of the books have resource kits that will give you additional ideas for teaching the material in the books.

The youth minister who takes advantage of training opportunities, encourages adults to attend, and provides training through the church can have a competent, informed team of adult leaders. Training is a vital part of the total youth ministry program. Loading up the church van with adult youth workers to attend a training event is just as much youth ministry as loading up that same van with high-school students going to camp.

Motivation and Support

Motivation is a key to maintaining your youth ministryleadership team. Your encouragement and affirmation can help keep youth workers on your team. A little public relations can be effective in showing support for those adults. Here are a couple of suggestions for showing that support.

Publicly affirm your adult leaders.—That affirmation can be an informal situation in the hallway with teenagers around. Or it can be a more specific formal situation such as a worship service where you commend the leaders for their contribution to a specific youth ministry project. Always be attentive to ways to say positive things about the adults who work with the youth.

Send thank you notes regularly.—Some obvious occasions suggest sending notes. You certainly would want to send notes of thanks to adults who help as camp counselors or possibly help serve at a youth banquet. However, be sensitive to thank people for what might seem to be insignificant things such as weekly workers meeting or for staying in the church parking lot until the last young person has gone home after a youth fellowship. Those acknowledgments will communicate to adults that you are paying close attention and appreciate all of their efforts.

Consider some kind of formal recognition for youth workers.—This could be a framed certificate presented annually to workers or maybe a banquet given in their honor to express appreciation.

Be visible in program organization activities.—Many ongoing youth program organization meetings and events may not require your direct leadership. As youth minister, however, your presence at these events demonstrates how much you value these ongoing programs, their leaders, and the youth who attend. Having you attend a regular meeting may go a long way to encourage the adults who provide leadership. A short visit to an Acteens slumber party or an occasional appearance at youth choir would not only build good relationships with teenagers but will communicate to the adultleaders that you are concerned and support their efforts.

Provide adult leaders all they need to do their jobs well.—A request for audiovisual equipment, art supplies, or bus/van reservation are just a few examples of the needs you can fill. Being assigned a task and not being provided the materials to complete the job is frustrating. As you are sensitive to the needs of your workers, they will be assured of your support.

At budget request time a good way to show support is to request money that can be used to provide for needs program leaders have brought to your attention. When adults observe that their needs are priorities in your budget plans, they know that program organization, leaders, and youth are all important to you.

Personal Ministry

The youth minister needs to be aware not only of needs for program supplies but also of needs for ministry among adult leaders. Your ministry to adult leaders models the kind of ministry they can have to teenagers in your church. Deaths or illnesses are obvious opportunities for ministry. But just as you grieve with them in death you can celebrate with them in the birth of a child or grandchild or when a child graduates from high school or college. Birthdays and anniversaries are also excellent times for you to communicate a personal word of love and support.

In some situations you may find yourself to be the counselor for those adults who work with you in youth ministry. Youth workers are not exempt from the problems of divorce, depression, and spiritual emptiness. As their youth minister, you might be the only one they would consider trusting at these tender times.

Taking the time and effort to develop a first-class group of youth workers can be one of your best investments. Take specific steps today that will get you to that point. Set aside time in your calendar each week that will be used exclusively to enlist, motivate, and minister to your adult youth workers.

---

[1]Daniel O. Aleshire, *Understanding Today's Youth* (Nashville: Convention Press, 1982).

[2]Merton Strommen, *Five Cries of Youth, Revised* (New York: Harper & Row, 1988).

[3]Richard Ross, compiler, *The 24-Hour Counselor* tape series (Nashville: Broadman, 1988); Richard Ross and Judi Hayes, authors-compiler, *Ministry with Youth in Crisis* (Nashville: Convention Press, 1988).

PERSONAL LEARNING ACTIVITIES

1. What kinds of adults make good youth workers?

2. Where can a youth minister find training opportunities for youth workers?

3. How can a youth minister show support to adult workers?

4. When do adult workers need the personal attention of the minister of youth?

CHAPTER 7

THE MINISTER OF YOUTH'S WORK WITH PARENTS

"As a parent, what do you expect from your youth minister?"

"I want him to motivate my youth spiritually."

"I would like her to convince my daughter not to date the boy she's been dating."

"Our son was given a soft drink at school with a drug in it. He became critically ill and was hospitalized for some time. Throughout the ordeal we never saw or heard from our youth minister. Was it too much to expect from him at least to call us."

"I want her to tell me how to communicate with my daughter as she does."

"Things are tight for us financially right now. I wish he would be more considerate by planning some things that don't cost as much."

Ministry to parents is more than meeting their expectations. But taking a look at just a

Dave Fuller
Director of youth education and ethnic and language religious education
Baptist General Convention of the State of Oklahoma
Oklahoma City, Oklahoma

sample of what they do expect begins to open windows to their perceptions of youth ministry and to their needs and those of their children.

Accepting the Challenge

During the past few years youth ministers have recognized the urgency of ministry to parents. Many youth ministries now include some programming for parents, a newsletter, and possibly counseling and support groups. However, some have discovered that ministry with parents is not simple and change is not immediate.

At the outset of developing a ministry to parents, the minister of youth should try to conceptualize a philosophy and theology of this kind of ministry. Seeking the counsel of those who have been involved in parents ministry will reveal a wide array of opinions and ministry experiences and opportunities.

An increasing number of youth ministers are parents of youth, but most are not. Relating to a teenager at church can be different from living with that same teenager at home. Coordinating a ministry to parents without having reared a teenager can be challenging. A few parents may even question whether a younger staff member should move into this role.

Mike Yaconelli wrote:

> I have been a youth worker for 25 years. For 21 of those years I was convinced that youth workers had a lot of great insights for parents of high school kids. There were many . . . who, I was convinced, were making terrible mistakes with their children. *If only they would listen to me,* I thought, *I know exactly what they should do.*
>
> For the last four years, at least one of my two boys has been in high school. Now I am not so sure those parents should have listened to me. Frankly, I am embarrassed that I thought parenting was so simple and clear cut. I am embarrassed that I entertained the notion that I could do a better job of parenting than most of the parents I was working with.[1]

The ever-changing structure of the modern family also makes ministry to parents a challenge. Ministers of youth cannot necessarily depend on the experiences in their own families of ori gin to help them understand the families from which their youth come.[2] Generally, experts seem to agree that by the year 2000 fewer than one half of the families in America will be traditional in the sense of children living with both biological parents.

All this is not intended to be discouraging but to help ministers of youth see ministry to parents as complex yet vital. Keys to effective ministry to parents include sensitivity , academic and personal study of family issues, and an openness to learning directly from parents.

Even faithful youth spend just a few hours a week at church. Those same youth may spend more than one hundred hours a week at home. Also, the inherent dynamics of parent-child relationships result in parents' having major roles in shaping who their children will become. Any positive change in the home can have a significant impact on teenagers living there.

Understanding Parents

"Ever since our divorce, my son hasn't wanted to go to church. He says he doesn't fit in anymore. He went through a time when he blamed himself for our problems, and he seemed to pull away from any close relationship he had. He doesn't even seem to have close friends anymore."

Trained youth ministers likely have an understanding of the process of adolescent development. They know about the adjustments that must be made physically, emotionally, mentally, and spiritually for healthy maturation to take place.

The minister of youth may or may not know, however, that the same adjustments, at varying degrees, are necessary for the parents of youth. This period is often called mid-life crisis. Just as emerging adolescents are faced with physiological changes, their parents might themselves be dealing with changes.

At the same time that they are being parents to their children, they may face taking additional responsibility for their aging parents. Parents are becoming aware during this time that they are becoming older adults.

> The middle-aged adult's primary task is to achieve a mature philosophy of life. They are to let go of the acquired philosophy they borrowed as adolescents and formulate a

deeper, rationally and emotionally integrated view of the universe in faith. This comes at the time adolescents are themselves attempting to develop their first philosophy of life and can be a time of extreme conflict in the home. Youthful idealism will clash with mid-life realism, but the bad conflicts come when parents grow cynical in their outlook on life.[3]

Effective ministry to parents will depend on the youth minister's understanding of the parents with whom he is seeking to minister. He or she will need to keep open eyes and ears to occurrences that affect parents such as jobs ending, crisis in the extended family, illness. Stress for parents affects the relationships between parents and youth, which naturally affects the youth with whom you work.

Supporting During Crises

Understanding is only the beginning. The minister of youth must be equipped and available as a care-giver. That doesn't mean that every youth minister must have a Ph.D. in psychology to be effective. It does mean that he or she needs to be present in a crisis situation to encourage and support.

Richard Ross wrote in the preface of *Ministry with Youth in Crisis*:

> I am writing these lines while sitting in a courtroom. In a few minutes a concerned judge will make a decision that will affect the rest of a teenager's life. Gary is a freshman in my youth group at church. Today he will discover which of two divorced parents he will live with the rest of his adolescence.
>
> Today is a crisis day for Gary and for both of his parents. Because I am Gary's youth minister, today is an important date for me as well. Even though I am considered a part-time staff member, ministry during times of crisis has become a regular part of my work with youth and families.[4]

When crisis strikes a family, the youth minister should be one of the first persons in contact with the family. But what can you do once you step into a crisis situation? Ron Mahn, adolescent counselor, suggested that the youth minister can take some basic steps with parents and youth in a crisis, recognizing that dif ferent kinds of crises need different types of actions.

Be present.—Your presence is important. Remind them of God's presence. Help them to know that even though the outcome of the crisis may not be what they would like, God's presence is with them. God also works through the presence of others. The youth minister can rally support for the parents. Be sensitive in the timing, but encourage others to offer their presence and support.

Listen attentively.—The next step to take in the ministry process will be determined by needs you hear expressed.

Be discreet.—Information may be given to you in a crisis situation that does not need to be repeated even in confidential prayer circles.

Depending on the crisis, misinformation may be spread through the youth group. Facilitate the group's awareness of the crisis to prevent rumors. Consult with the parents to see what and how much information they want to be shared with the youth.[5]

Many families in crisis need the help of community professionals. The minister prepared to make good referrals can be a valuable help to families. (For more help in crisis intervention, see *Ministry with Youth in Crisis.*)

Reaching and Teaching Parents

"My wife and I grew up in different kinds of churches. When we got married, we couldn't agree on what kind of church to attend, so we quit going. I don't mind our daughter's going to church. Anything they can do to help her straighten out is fine with me."

In a typical youth group, a large percentage of the youth involved have parents who are not involved or do not even attend church. Moses, in speaking to the Israelites, seemed to indicate that the ideal place for Christian education is the home. Moses told the people, "These commandments that I give you today are to be upon your hearts. Impress them on your children. Talk about them when you sit at home and when you walk along the road, when you lie down and when you get up. Tie them as symbols on your hands and bind them on your foreheads. Write them on the door frames of your houses and on your gates"

(Deut. 6:6-9, NIV).[6]

Deuteronomy 6:20, NIV, continues, "In the future, when your son asks you, 'What is the meaning of the stipulations, decrees and laws the Lord our God has commanded you?' tell him." One of the most important ministries we can provide is to reach parents for Christ, help them grow as disciples, and teach them to nurture their children in the Lord.

Many ministers of youth provide regular training for parents. Here is an example excerpted from a newsletter for parents:

Prayer n' Share for Adults
More than 214 youth at our church have been trained to have a time alone with God. Beginning Sunday night, June 9, at 5:45, you can receive the same training they have had to establish or improve your daily devotional time.[7]

Coordination with other age-group leaders in the church, other program organizations, and the family life committee can strengthen ministry to parents. For example, Equipping Center modules, produced by the Discipleship Training Department of the Sunday School Board and available from Baptist Book Stores, are a superb training resource that can be offered through a church's ongoing Discipleship Training program. Here are a few of the modules that might be helpful in ministry to parents:

- *Discipleship in the Home*
- *Home: Key to Christian Values*
- *How to Lead Your Family in Bible Study and Worship*
- *Parent-Teen Relationships*
- *Caring in Times of Family Crisis*
- *Families Practicing God's Love*

Youth ministers can help motivate churches to provide for parents groups built around the Parenting by Grace materials.[8]

One of the most worthwhile ministries we can do for youth is to reach their lost parents. Evangelizing parents, however, can present a sensitive dilemma. Parents who are hostile toward the church can make their teenagers' participation in the church difficult.

More times than not, a relationship with parents will have to be developed in order to lead to a witnessing opportunity. The leaders in the appropriate adult class or department should become a part of the youth ministry team at this point by viewing these parents as evangelistic prospects, then seeking to involve them in the life of the church with other adults their age.

Communication with uninvolved parents can give them a sense a being a part of their youth's activities. Assume that all parents want to know about what the church is doing in the lives of their children.

Youth who have lost parents should be involved in the efforts to win their parents for Christ. When a parent is identified as being lost, set a time to meet with the youth of that parent to discuss his/her feelings about how to reach the parent. Many times youth will initiate the process by expressing concern for their lost parent(s).

Provide training for youth in how to share their faith with their parents. Providing this training in a group setting, comprised of youth whose parents are lost, can give encouragement and support for this unique group.

Becoming a Parent Advocate

"I need to feel the security of knowing the youth leader is treating the parent/child relationship with dignity and respect. He or she needs to reinforce my values with my children. He or she doesn't always have to agree with me, but he or she does need to reinforce what is good and right in my relationship with my child."[9]

In an article, "The Dynamic Duo: Teaming Up with Parents for More Effective Youth Ministry!", Rick Caldwell listed the "Ten Commandments for Ministering with Parents of Youth":

1. Expand the scope of your ministry to include parents.
2. Explain your strategy of ministry to parents.
3. Equip parents to reinforce your work with youth spiritually.
4. Educate parents on how to detect danger signs in their children.
5. Enlist parents to work in your ministry.
6. Experience life with your youth at home.
7. Exalt the role of the parent.

8. Enjoy fellowship with parents.
9. Encourage parents during times of crisis.
10. Evaluate your ministry with parents.[10]

Everyone who has worked with youth for any length of time will attest to the importance of spending time with youth in different kinds of settings. That is essential in knowing the youth with whom you work. Spending time with parents is no less important.

A round of golf with a father, or inviting parents to have lunch with you will not only give you a chance to affirm their son or daughter but will also provide a wealth of information about your youth's home life. Give them a chance to know you, your goals and objectives. And knowing the needs and concerns of parents will allow you to do the kind of programming for them in your ministry that will be most effective.

Planning That Meets Family Needs

We say that we are for the family. Yet many times we schedule youth activities so heavily that we create additional stress for the family and lessen the likelihood that they will spend time together.

One youth minister was asked by a parent, "When are you going to start taking our kids out for pizza after church like our other youth minister did?"

"I'm not. Why don't you take them? Going out to eat after church would be a good chance for you to be together as a family," was his response.

"Certainly youth leaders cannot control how families spend their lives. Healthy Christian leaders are helpers not controllers. The youth leader can help families spend time together by (1) making it logistically possible for families to find time to be together, (2) providing the motivation for families to be together, and (3) providing help in knowing how best to use time when together."[11]

Create times for youth and their parents to be together. A parent-youth retreat is an idea many have used successfully. Rather than always planning a Saturday night social event, give the youth ideas for a parents' night off. Give them a simple menu for preparing dinner for the family and ideas for family activities for the evening. (Additional ideas for parent-youth activities can be found in chapter 9 of *Ministry with Youth and Their Parents* by Richard Ross and Wade Rowatt.

Communicating with Parents

Helping parents be informed will affirm them and gain support for your ministry to youth. Newsletters to parents can be a good channel of communication by including promotion of youth programs, information about the world of youth, and opportunities for parents. Newsletters can also periodically list new resources available for parents.

Communication between youth and parents is always near the top of the list of both parents and youth when listing needs of the family. Training and resources to strengthen communication should be a part of every youth ministry.

Good communication is one characteristic of a healthy family. Unfortunately, communication skills don't always come naturally. In a parent-youth relationship, many times emotions run high, which complicates communication even more. Youth and parents alike need help and practice in communicating at three basic levels: (1) giving and receiving information, (2) sharing emotions, and (3) communicating nonverbally.[12]

Again, as parents and their youth participate in opportunities to communicate that you have provided, they will begin to improve their communication skills.

Supporting Parents

"My teenage son is making the adjustment to having a stepfather, although not as quickly as I would like. The first time the two of them were at home alone together, they got into an argument. My son left home. Fortunately, the first person he went to was our youth minister. He was able to get my husband and son together to talk through the problem."

Seek to provide opportunities for parents to talk with one another. The youth minister can provide a support network for parents by establishing parent support groups and scheduling parents meetings where they can discuss needs, problems, frustration, and advice. Many youth ministers refer to this as a parents' roundtable. Other meetings can spotlight community professionals who have information or support that parents need.

This kind of meeting makes a good first-time parents meeting because, as you listen attentively, you will hear needs surface which will provide the basis for future programming. Parents find real support in hearing other parents verbalize the frustrations, challenges, and good times in raising teenagers.

Parent support groups can be established by enlisting parents who have worked through some of the dilemmas typically faced by families with teenagers to serve as a resource of encouragement to others facing similar problems. Obviously, you will need to seek out those who don't mind talking openly and honestly about their particular journeys. A resource group like this might include a single parent, parents who have worked through a teenage pregnancy or a substance abuse crisis or some other problem.

Ask this group to serve as a panel for a parents meeting. This will give you an opportunity to introduce the group to the kind of support that is available. Let parents know whom they might call for assistance. (*Living with Teenagers* magazine includes in each issue specific guidance for parent support groups.)

Becoming a Resource for Parents

"We are active in church; but as our daughter gets older, I see her losing interest in church. I see the same thing happening to the older youth I work with in Sunday School. I realize that it is not the youth minister's sole responsibility to keep our youth motivated and involved, but I don't know what else to do."

Merton Strommen, reporting on extensive research done with younger adolescents and their parents, explained that both youth and their parents desire to work as a family to grow in faith. The research showed, however, that few families spend time talking about the subject at home.

"When asked, 'How often does your family sit down together and talk about God, the Bible . . . or other religious things?' 42 percent of the younger adolescents say this never happens; 32

percent say this topic is discussed once or twice a month, 13 percent say it is discussed once a week. And this . . . is the finding from a survey of largely church-connected families, of whom 97 percent are members of a church."[13]

The youth minister's effectiveness will be enhanced as he or she is aware of resources that are available in the church. If planned family ministries are not a part of the ongoing church program, the youth minister can take some initiative to create the awareness of such programs.

Ministry with parents take time. Youth ministers already struggling with heavy schedules may wonder where time for new ministries will come from. The solution is found in chapter 4, "The Minister of Youth's Philosophy of Youth Ministry." Many youth ministers are beginning to commit one third of their work hours to ministry with and for parents.

This shift may mean programming a little less for youth. Many youth ministers are willing to make this shift because of the potential ministry with parents represents. Indeed, ministry with parents is youth ministry. It is simply a ministry to youth through those who shape so much of their lives.

Most youth ministers can't work any more hours a week. However, they can spend those hours doing the things that matter most.

Ministry to parents is crucial. The breadth and intensity of the ministry will depend on factors such as skills and knowledge of the minister to youth, time and resources available, and the direction and commitment of the church.

Resources are available to aid the youth minister in designing and developing a ministry to parents. Other youth ministers are glad to share their successes and failures. Conferences are available to train ministers in many aspects of family ministry.

To be successful, a philosophy of parent ministry must be established, priorities set, and strategies developed.

---

[1]Mike Yaconelli, "Synchro-Mesh Ministry: The Parent-Youth Worker Connection," *Youthworker*, Spring 1985, 20-21.

[2]Richard Ross and G. Wade Rowatt, Jr., *Ministry with Youth and Their Parents* (Nashville: Convention Press, 1986), 13.

[3]Ibid., 30.

[4]Richard Ross and Judi Hayes, comp., *Ministry with Youth in Crisis* (Nashville: Convention Press, 1988), 5.

[5]Ron Mahn of Oklahoma City, interview by author, 21 October 1988.

[6]From the Holy Bible, *New International Version*, copyright © 1973, 1978, 1984 by International Bible Society.

[7]*Parent-A-Gram*, newsletter of First Baptist Church, Geyer Springs, Little Rock, Arkansas.

[8]For more information on Parenting by Grace materials, write Family Ministry Department, 127 Ninth Avenue, North, Nashville, TN 37234 or check your *Church Materials Catalog.*

[9]Marlene LeFever, "And the Score Is . . . Parents Rate Their Youth Workers," *Youthworker*, Spring 1985, 28.

[10]Rick Caldwell, "The Dynamic Duo: Teaming Up with Parents for More Effective Youth Ministry!" *equipping youth*, April 1984, 34.

[11]Ross and Rowatt, 74.

[12]Ibid., 45.

[13]Merton P. and A. Irene Strommen, *Five Cries of Parents* (San Francisco: Harper and Row, 1985), 133-34.

PERSONAL LEARNING ACTIVITES

1. What societal changes have led to the need for a youth minister to minister to parents of youth?

2. When should a minister of youth seek to minister to parents?

3. Suggest some helpful resources.

4. Suggest activities for parents a youth minister can plan.

CHAPTER 8

THE MINISTER OF YOUTH'S ADMINISTRATIVE AND PLANNING SKILLS

For many youth ministers, just the thought of planning and administrative responsibility conjures up terrible thoughts of boring, confining busywork that never amounts to anything. Well, I want to let you in on a little secret. Although we often may think that planning is usually the death rattle of creativity, you've probably been planning all along. Remember that stroke-of-genius idea you had a while back that resulted in the best youth retreat your church ever had? Now, think back to what it took to move that idea from just another "what if" to the reality of young lives being changed on a retreat. All of the steps involved different elements of planning. While that planning may not have been in the form of reams of calendar pages or lifeless meetings, it was, nevertheless, planning and hard work that made a successful event.

Bill Falkner
Church Training
Associate
Arkansas Baptist
State Convention
Little Rock, Arkansas

Much is being said these days about the youth minister as a professional. Granted, the idea of "professional" may have a negative image when compared to the person-centered touch of ministry. *Professional* does include , however, the positive concept of responsible and committed stewardship of limited resources. Good planning and administrative skills are vital tools that move us forward in touching lives and developing people.

This chapter is designed to help you focus on the importance of planning and administration as part of the work and calling of youth ministry. We will be looking at concepts and ideas more than samples of calendars and budgets. The resources containing those kinds of helps will be pointed out as we go along.

The Ministry of Administration

If we were to strip away all the personal, emotional, and spiritual elements of youth ministry and examine what is left, we would see a relatively common sight. We would see, essentially, a small business based on the use of relatively limited resources such as people, time, money. Obviously, depending on your church, that business comparison may be more like a weekend hot-dog stand or a rapidly growing corporation. Whatever the size, the truth remains that a person or persons are needed to make that business accomplish its purpose.

A typical youth minister response at this point might be, "But God didn't call me to be a bookkeeper or personnel director or manager. He called me to minister to people." This may be true, but we are not alone in this dilemma. A biblical character of old experienced a similar frustration.

In Exodus 18, we find Moses faced with the problem of personally handling all disputes or quarrels that arose among the people. Moses' father-in-law, Jethro, saw the trap in which Moses was snared and offered a practical solution. Jethro basically told Moses to be an administrator in order to fulfill God's purpose for Moses as well as for the Hebrew children. By delegating a portion of his responsibility through other people, Moses was better able to accomplish God's purpose for him as a minister and leader. Such a simple suggestion saved Moses from potential burnout and a grossly overwhelming task. Sounds like a typical church staff situation, doesn't it?

Several timely truths from this story warrant our attention. We easily can become so overwhelmed by the intricacies of human relations, particularly when they involve teenagers, that we are unable to do adequately the task to which we have been called. The same was true for Moses. He became so inundated by the sheer volume of concerns that Jethro saw him rapidly moving toward ineffectiveness.

Regarding administration, four main truths stand out from Moses' experience:

Showing concern for persons.—Obviously, Moses was conscientious about dealing with the problems of his people. His abilities and effectiveness, however, were multiplied as he worked through others. An important lesson in ministry is learned when we feel free to enable and equip others to accomplish a common goal.

Operating from strengths.—Jethro helped Moses discover his strengths not just as a good and wise listener but also as an enabler and multiplier of others. An important key to being a good administrator is to discover and develop an effective style of leadership. Some people are thinkers, and others are riskers. We may be theoretical or practical in our thinking and dependent or independent in our risking. Many tools and instruments are available to help identify and develop leadership styles. The Church Administration Department of the Sunday School Board offers many training events on state and national levels to help ministers develop as leaders and administrators.

Money budgeted for professional training and personal growth can provide the financial support for such experiences. A week spent at Glorieta or Ridgecrest Baptist Conference Centers or one of the occasional national youth ministry conferences can be a positive experience in discovering and further developing leadership strengths.

Managing time.—Another benefit of this lesson in basic administration came in Jethro's insistence that Moses wisely manage his time. Moses had more to do with his time than just serve as arbitrator and referee. He had many other responsibilities that may have been less obvious but no less important.

One of the greatest challenges in the life of a youth minister is the management of time—both personally and professionally. A seminary professor often described serving on a church staff as "a ministry of interruptions." The minister's time often is seen as a universal invitation to visit or recreate at anyone's whim. The constant tension between the need for structure and spontaneity is real and at times seemingly relentless. Further attention to time management will be emphasized when we look at planning and professionalism.

Developing a strong team concept.—The modern-day equivalent of Jethro's advice to Moses would be an interoffice memo which boldly declares, "Hey, this isn't a one-man show; we're all in this together."

The development of a sense of team which includes youth, parents, and leaders is second only to a personal relationship with Christ in youth ministry. In the book *Shared Ministry: A Journey Toward Togetherness in Ministry*, we find a blueprint for the biblical mode of the ministry team—the church.[1] By sharing the ministry with everyone involved, we not only multiply our effectiveness; but we also open the door to invaluable opportunities for growth and nurture.

Some Planning Tips for Effective Ministry

A trip to your nearest Baptist Book Store confirms the fact that many books, workbooks, and guides relate to some area of planning. The most practical and helpful planning guide for youth ministry is *Youth Ministry Planbook 4.*[2] Complete with step-by-step helps for calendar and budget planning, this planning tool is a must for every youth minister.

Every youth minister has his or her own pet ideas related to planning. Like Moses, much of how we plan is based on who we are and who we model. Several general principles for effective planning follow:

Planning should grow out of needs.—The key to Christ's earthly ministry was His powerful sense of people's needs. An effective youth ministry must reflect and respond to the needs of youth, parents, and leaders as well as the church as a whole.

While talking about needs may be easy, discerning and un

derstanding those needs is a much more difficult matter. Open, honest communication is usually a great place to start. Listening sessions, brainstorming, dialogue, and informal conversations can reveal volumes about needs within a particular youth group, church, or community. A survey instrument such as the *Shared Ministry Youth Survey* can provide keen insight to the perceived needs of the youth ministry.[3] Again, *Youth Ministry Plan Book 4* contains specific guidance on how to implement needs-based planning.

Planning must involve others.—Much like the variety of needs which exist in any youth group, that same group consists of youth of varying maturity levels, intelligence, and potential. Planning which focuses on developing the full potential of each youth as well as the group will naturally involve other people.

A time-tested rule of thumb in youth ministry is to enlist one helper for each five youth anticipated to attend a youth event. That means that in order to reach a goal of one hundred at the after-game fellowship, at least 20 people need to be involved in the various levels of planning and conducting that event. Not only does such involvement help ensure a larger number, but also it provides practical experience for leadership development and affirmation.

Planning should be realistic.—Most youth ministers have been asked at some point why their church can't do youth activities like the big church up the road. Of course, we know that we could do all those neat activities if we had the same $70,000 youth ministry budget!

Obviously, the point here is to be realistic in planning. Our planning should be within the reasonable bounds of finances, leadership, time, and other resources available. As a youth minister discovers needs and involves others, the natural progression will be to be more realistic in what is actually planned and implemented.

We all know that it helps for a youth minister to be just a little spontaneous and creative when planning a great way to minister to youth. But that same spontaneity or just plain desire to do all we can sometimes becomes our potential downfall. For example, almost all youth ministers have found themselves saying something like: "That's a great idea for a retreat. We'll plan to have that this spring." Of course, nothing is wrong with projecting and planning a spring retreat, unless it is in addition to the DiscipleNow Weekend, youth revival, and WOW school planned within that same time frame. We can easily get caught up in the excitement of planning a large number of activities and emphases and then suddenly realize that more is planned than we can ever accomplish. This may be a particular trap to avoid if you are involved in setting goals and objectives as a part of some performance review criteria. What might appear to impress a personnel committee on paper could be later seen as a failure because it was not realistic in terms of time, budget, or some other criteria.

Planning should be supportive.—A few years ago a gifted youth minister left a church in our state to take a similar position in another church. The pastor of that new church said that what most attracted him to this youth minister was the fact that he was "willing to color outside the lines." Such bold creativity and nontraditional approaches were obvious strengths and gifts in this person's ministry.

About two years later, I received a call stating that this same youth minister who rapidly had built an impressive ministry reaching hundreds of youth had been asked to leave and was seeking a new position. Later I discovered the real problem. The pastor who had been so impressed with this youth minister found that what he thought was just creativity turned out to be more lone-ranger youth ministry than anything else. The youth minister insisted on pursuing his own course without any recognition of other areas of the youth division such as Youth Sunday School, Youth Discipleship Training, Youth Choir, and youth missions education organizations. In fact, the primary complaint lodged against this person was that he refused to be a part of the church staff ministry team.

Although the above example is admittedly extreme, it does point out the need for balance and support in planning. Such planning should involve program leaders in Youth Sunday School, Discipleship Training, music, Acteens, and Pioneers and High School Baptist Young Men. Of course, the best way to in volve these organizations is through representation on the Youth Ministry Council. *The Youth Ministry Council Guidebook* provides excellent, detailed steps for training this important planning and support team.[4]

In addition to those already mentioned, supportive planning should also include appropriate input from the Church Council, deacons, or other coordinating groups. Not only does this method provide valuable input and direction from many sources, but also it develops a strong sense of team work in youth ministry. Teamwork changes parents and leaders from adversaries and competitors to partners and friends. Teamwork changes a church staff from a bunch of personalities to a fine-tuned combination of God-blessed gifts and talents capable of leading a church to reach its fullest potential. And best of all, it changes youth ministry from a short-term, bag-of-tricks show to a vibrant process of touching lives with God's love and being a part of that metamorphosis.

A Potpourri of Pointers for a Permanently Positive Ministry

To this point we have examined several fairly broad and logical principles of sound administration and planning. Obviously, to stop here would leave more than a few stones unturned and would justifiably make many youth ministers ask, "Where are the practical, nitty-gritty handles I need to do more than just survive?"

Through the course of several years of service on local church staffs and over a decade on the state denominational level, I have been able to observe and be a part of the work of many youth ministers. Becoming a professional youth minister may be one of the most important goals a youth minister can have. If we, for just a moment, can ignore the negative emotions elicited by that word *professional*, we might be able to see more positive connotations than negative. A professional in any field is often thought of as one whose seriousness about and commitment to a vocational choice goes beyond a mere job and strives for higher goals. In the business world this has been best described as the search for excellence.

If the secular world considers excellence to be a worthy goal, how much more should the excellence portrayed by Christ Himself be the driving force of the professional youth minister. The professional youth minister should have several recognizable qualities and disciplines in ministry:

Keeping regular office hours is important.—No, this does not mean a chain cuffed to your leg and welded to the desk. Some regularity of office hours should provide for consistent contact with people. They should also be flexible enough to allow for late hours, long periods of work, stress, and personal and family needs. In other words, office hours are a communication tool. Your consistent presence in the office may communicate competence, stewardship, and commitment. Your absence may communicate unconcern, suspicion, and laziness.

Looking professional will help others to see you as a professional.—The harsh truth is that if you are a youth minister, you are just that—not a youth. Professional youth ministers should dress appropriately to their age and to the demands of the occasion. That does not mean three-piece suits at youth camp, but it does mean that the youth minister should not wear inappropriate attire in violation of a dress code. Yes, at times a suit is appropriate attire even for the youth minister.

Acting professional is needed, too.—The area of personal habits is also a prime concern to many churches. We all are aware of gifted ministers whose effectiveness and credibility have been instantly destroyed by personal sin and inconsistencies. The youth minister does live in a glass house of sorts. Our personal habits should be those that allow us to be human while uplifting and glorifying the name of the One we serve.

The professional youth minister also manages resources wisely.—We all struggle with time management. Time has been called the common denominator of all humanity. We all have the same amount of time each day. The nature of ministry is giving, and youth ministry can also take time from self and family. Without a doubt, balance is needed.

Many excellent books and other resources are available which detail effective time management systems. The secret, however, is not how rigidly we adhere to a system but rather what tool we use to manage our time. A simple "to do" list on a daily basis is probably the most practical. Such a tool helps to keep us on task and avoid unproductive dead time.

A filing system which meets your ministry needs and goals is another helpful tool. An important rule to remember in filing is to keep it simple. A cumbersome, detailed filing system becomes a barrier rather than a help; simplicity and practicality are worthy goals.

Managing resources wisely also applies to self-control. A wise deacon gave me some valuable advice early in my ministry. He said, "The two things that will ruin your ministry are misuse of morals and misuse of money." How accurate and true his words are.

Youth ministers are uniquely vulnerable to situations that might lead to moral indiscretions. Sometimes a situation is misinterpreted and shared through gossip. Other times extra attention given to a troubled young person may cause a problem. An extra amount of caution can help prevent the possibility of gossip or of a problem situation and can add to the youth minister's image as a professional. Our entire effectiveness and credibility as ministers depends on moral consistency.

The second half of that deacon's advice is more subtle but just as true. A minister who has a reputation for financial irresponsibility is, at best, a joke in the community and, at worst, an outright hypocrite. A necessary but unfortunate trend among church search committees is to run a credit check, along with the usual references, on a prospective staff member. Encouraging sound personal money management is not an excuse for some churches to pay low salaries; rather, it is a call to personal integrity and high ministry standards for every minister.

Professional ministers of youth maintain good relationships with all church staff members.—Most of the church problems that result in a split or serious break of fellowship are not centered in a weighty matter of theology or doctrine but usually are found in some problem with relationships. Such problems seem to be particularly intense when found within a church office or staff. Among other problems which result from staff discord, common knowledge of division within the church staff causes difficulty in counseling with youth and their parents.

At the risk of sounding simplistic and idealistic, the universal cure for relational problems is open communication built on common respect for each person's abilities and contributions to ministry. Through this perspective, a healthy concept of shared ministry is developed. Jealousy and lack of understanding of ministry roles, which are often sources of conflict and resentment, can be reduced through shared ministry.

Disagreements will develop among a church staff or office personnel. How we respond to those disagreements is the key. Can we respond in an attitude of love, respect, and forgiveness? If this is the attitude, we truly can become effective models from which our youth can see truth and love personified.

Avoid common errors.—Just as a professional youth minister can learn to do certain things to become more competent, some behaviors must be avoided. Even the most creative, gifted youth minister can be virtually destroyed by four seemingly simple but potentially deadly errors:

- Consistently doing things late.
- Consistently operating over budget.
- Consistently failing to return calls.
- Consistently failing to carry through on requests.

These may seem trivial, but if you frequently do any or all of these, you may already be in trouble! Remember that the goal is not to be the perfect administrator; rather, the goal is to be the youth minister who wisely develops and uses good administrative skills.

Use the Youth Ministry Council.—I occasionally hear youth ministers complain that the Youth Ministry Council is just an ineffective waste of time. An interesting fact usually emerges almost universally in those complaints. Most of the youth ministers who voice this complaint tend to have relatively short tenure in the churches they serve. Granted, they may have 18 years of youth ministry behind them, but many will have spent them in 9 or 10 churches. Usually the long-tenured youth minister of 8, 10, or more years in the same church can boast about the effectiveness of a Youth Ministry Council.

A youth ministry of interdependency strengthens all the programs and helps a youth minister avoid the pitfalls of working alone. As Paul encouraged the early church to rejoice in one another's victories and grieve in one another's sorrow, so should we see our youth ministries strengthened through working together as a team.

Don't forget the last step of any youth event. Although great effort may be expended on a single event or emphasis, we typically spend little if any time evaluating the event. Evaluation is like history; failure to learn its lessons dooms us to repeat its mistakes.

The main barrier to evaluation is usually time. We may be in such a rush to move on to the next item or event that we simply choose not to evaluate the one just completed. Effective evaluation does not have to be a cumbersome process. The process can be a simple written questionnaire circulated at the end of an activity. Or it can be a listening session with youth, parents, and leaders. The bottom line in evaluation is a positive communication of the desire to make every facet of youth ministry one that helps youth and glorifies God.

The Final Keys to Success

A logical question at this point might be, How can I be the efficient, effective administrator/planner that I need to be? Consider these ideas as seeds in search of fertile ground:

Let you be you.—One of the greatest triumphs in any minister's life is facing a mirror and feeling generally satisfied with the reflection. This is a cause for celebration! God created us with the desire to be whole and in balance with Him.

Sometimes the pressure and grind of ministry robs us of our uniqueness and potential. God has given you permission to be you—not some unrealistic fabrication of perfection. You can and should be that real human being capable of laughter and hurt, exhilaration and fatigue, faith and doubt. A neat desk, complete calendar, or balanced budget does not make you the best administrator/planner. The real key is your own uniqueness, guided by the Spirit, resulting in changed lives.

Get in touch.—A popular TV news show always ends with the reminder to be in touch. We need to develop a keen awareness and understanding of our own skills, gifts, and potentials.

Self-examination and introspection often bear the fruit of personal growth and achievement.

Youth ministry is also strengthened by a youth minister who is in touch with the latest in administrative resources and approaches. A firm understanding of your own strengths and weaknesses is a positive step toward personal and professional maturity.

Develop a plan.—No goal is ever reached without some measure of planning. Even Christ modeled a plan as He moved toward loving redemption on Calvary. Planning carries more significance than being merely the key ingredient in creating a successful event. Planning communicates the full purpose and intensity which surrounds the essence of call.

Have a good time.—God intends for youth ministry to be more service than sentence, more people than process, and more enjoyment than endurance. When administrative detail can be seen as the means to growing youth, helping parents, and developing leaders, then all the work and effort is worthwhile. Planning that goes beyond squares on a page and results in committed youth is one of ministry's sweetest treats. In short, avoid being buried by guilt and frustrated by failures. Instead, do today what you can with what you have for Jesus' sake and have a good time!

Administrative and planning skills for the youth minister should not be considered as just another tool of ministry but rather one which fulfills the biblical admonition of "decency and order" while providing freedom and structure for effective ministry.

The role of the youth minister as administrator is a hat which helps place us in the unique position of the servant/leader. Administration combines the many facets of enabling, equipping, and encouraging into effective stewardship of time and other resources.

Think of administration as an investment process—hours and energy spent in planning, conducting, and evaluating. Administration is also an investment in trust—trusting others as well as self. Now think of the return on those investments. Quality administration is measured not only in dollars but more likely in lives—the lives of leaders, parents, and youth who are recipients of and participants in a balanced youth ministry. What better arena exists in which to translate the seemingly mundane details of administration and planning than in the lives of those touched by an effective youth ministry.

---

[1]Joe R. Stacker and Bruce Grubbs, compilers, *Shared Ministry: A Journey Toward Togetherness in Ministry* (Nashville: Convention, 1985).

[2]Richard Ross, compiler, *Youth Ministry Planbook 4* (Nashville: Convention, 1989).

[3]*Shared Ministry: Basic Packet*; *Shared Ministry: Interpretation Packet*; and *Shared Ministry: Survey Instruments Packet* are available on the Undated Materials Order Form or by calling 1-800-458-BSSB. For more information, write Youth Ministry, Sunday School Board, 127 Ninth Avenue, North, Nashville, TN 37234.

[4]Richard Ross, *Youth Ministry Council Guidebook* (Nashville: Convention, 1987).

PERSONAL LEARNING ACTIVITIES

1. Discuss four concepts about planning that youth ministers can learn from Moses and Jethro.

2. Discuss several general planning principles, and apply them to your church.

3. What is a simple rule to follow in knowing how many adults are needed to plan and implement a youth event?

4. Name several areas in which a youth minister should be a professional.

5. What are some pitfalls a youth minister should avoid?

CHAPTER 9

THE MINISTER OF YOUTH'S ROLE WITH THE DENOMINATION

Southern Baptists enjoy a rich heritage. Youth ministers, as persons committed to God and identified as a legitimate part of the ministering team, should also be actively involved in a supportive relationship with our Convention. Youth ministers then may rightly be confronted with the question, "What role are you taking in the denomination?"

Check your response to this question by evaluating your own role with the denomination. Circle your most appropriate response for each statement.

Jerry Pounds
Associate professor of religious education
New Orleans Baptist Theological Seminary
New Orleans, Louisiana

SA   A   U   D   SD

strongly agree agree undecided disagree strongly disagree

1. I pray daily for my denomination and its leaders.

SA   A   U   D   SD

2. I speak good words of my associational,

state, and denomination-wide youth leaders.

SA   A   U   D   SD

3. I am considered by others to be a strong supporter of the activities in my association.

SA   A   U   D   SD

4. I support my associational youth committee by leading my youth to attend events.

SA   A   U   D   SD

5. I meet regularly with local youth ministers in my area for prayer, fellowship, and support.

SA   A   U   D   SD

6. I accept leadership opportunities in my association or state.

SA   A   U   D   SD

7. I budget an adequate amount of money to attend denominational events.

SA   A   U   D   SD

8. I support the denomination by using ongoing curriculum and leadership materials with my youth, leaders, and parents.

SA   A   U   D   SD

9. I attend associational, state, or national Convention-wide youth leadership training events.

SA   A   U   D   SD

10. I can identify all national youth leaders in our denomination.

SA   A   U   D   SD

Give yourself a score of 5 for every "strongly agree" statement; 4 for the "agree" statements; 3 for the "undecided" statements; 2 for the "disagree" statements; and 1 for the "strongly disagree" statements. Write your total score here: _____

If your total score fell between 45 and 50, you should be proud of your "denominational development." You are an effective model for other youth ministers and members of your church. A score of 40-45 indicates an overall positive role you play in the denomination. You can identify your strengths and recognize areas for improvement. A score of 35-40 shows tendencies for you to be supportive in some denominational areas but with room for additional involvement. A score of 30 or below should remind you that you can be more involved in associational, state, and Convention-wide youth opportunities. You can become the beneficiary and supplier of rich experiences.

Evaluating Problems and Potentials

Some youth ministers are not more involved with the denomination for a number of reasons. Some reasons are based on bad experiences in the past, while others stem from poor or negative modeling by their own youth minister. In any case, people have reasons for not getting involved. Consider the following problems and potentials:

Ignorance

Problem.—For some unknowing youth ministers, their lack of involvement with the denomination is based purely on what they know, or rather what they don't know. They demonstrate a basic lack of knowledge about what is available to them.

Potential.—Contact youth ministers in your area to find out the ministries/activities in which you and your church can become involved. Set up a meeting with your director of missions or state youth consultant. Don't further penalize yourself by not knowing.

Laziness

Problem.— Some youth ministers capitalize on their laziness and disguise it by appearing too busy to get involved. Likely, this problem is not only affected by what is not done in the denomination but also by what is not done in their own churches. The trait is probably also evident in other areas of these persons' lives.

Potential.—Examine your sense of calling. Your laziness may be, in reality, a lived-out frustration of not being where God has called you. Put forth the effort and demonstrate the meaning of personal integrity.

Time

Problem.—On the surface this problem seems to be legitimate. Who honestly has time to do all we want or need to do? The reason for not having time to get involved, however, may be a camouflage for poor time management. We normally do what we feel is important, and we find the time to do it.

Potential.—Evaluate how you spend your time every day. You may need to learn how to prioritize your time better. In this way, the insignificant does not monopolize your quality time.

Fitting In

Problem.—Most of us have experienced the hollow feeling of not fitting in a group. We're either left out or made not to belong. Our normal reaction is to withdraw and find contentment within ourselves. By doing this, we fail to involve ourselves with others.

Potential.—Realize that every person is made uniquely by God, and by His own design we are different. By involving yourself with a group, you bring your own uniqueness to its attention. Take the initiative to fit in.

Fear

Problem.—The unwarranted fear is that we might lose our identity by cooperating with other youth ministers. We may fear competition, adventure, or failure.

Potential.—In this case, fear may be of the unknown. The simple principle is that the more we risk, the more comfortable we are to risk again. Taking the first step in involvement diminishes the barrier of fear.

Bad Memories

Problem.—Some youth ministers have memories of weak denominational youth events. They may have been embarrassed when their youth received little of value. They may have found getting youth to go to other events difficult.

Potential.—Do you have a heart for teenagers outside your church? Remember that for most smaller churches, associational and state youth events represent virtually all of the specialized youth ministry their teenagers will receive. Strong church youth ministers who pull their expertise, enthusiasm, and budget out of denominational youth events virtually guarantee those events will be mediocre.

By committing your skills and resources to associational and state events, you can significantly strengthen a ministry that will bless not only your youth but many others, too.

"Me-ism"

Problem.—Unfortunately, this problem is common to some youth ministers. The verbal message sounds like, "It's not worth my effort," or, "It doesn't meet my needs." Basically, the behavior shows a need for no one. The "me-ism" problem says that in order to have an effective youth ministry I must not rely on others but do everything myself.

Potential.—What a wonderful lesson to be learned by supporting the work of other youth ministers! You need them as much as they need you. A mutual cooperation benefits all involved.

Read 1 Corinthians 3:1-9. Now read the paragraph below and react to the two questions at the end.

The tendency for some youth ministers today is to seek to accomplish ministry apart from anyone else. Their "Apollos" or "Paul" has become recognition, pride, boasting, or even budget, numbers, or facilities. The tragedy is to seek to accomplish the efforts with the exclusion of any attempt to work with other youth ministers. We need to be reminded that God has gifted each of us to accomplish His purpose of reaching a lost world and that no youth minister has reason for personal glory or boasting.

Can you identify an additional reason youth ministers do not involve themselves more in the denomination?

Exploring the Possibilities

In 1947, a young shepherd boy followed one of his goats along a rocky mountainside. There the boy saw a cliff with a cave entrance, and his curiosity was more than he could handle. Dreaming of treasure he threw a rock into the cave. After hearing his stone crash into pottery, he investigated further and found jars, some broken and some intact, against the side of the cave.

Excited, he found a friend; and the two boys entered the cave.

However, instead of finding gold and silver, they found old leather and rags.

A cobbler in Bethlehem soon took these seemingly worthless finds off their hands. To make a long story short, these scrolls and many others eventually found their way into the hands of scholars. The young shepherd boy had not known actually how priceless his discovery was as these were the Dead Sea Scrolls.

Perhaps you haven't explored the possibilities and benefits of becoming more involved with our denomination. Consider these benefits and claim an incredible treasure waiting to be discovered.

By being involved with our denomination, you will be able to:

Broaden your base of ministry.—Your philosophy of ministry should have for its target your own local church. But does it have other churches in mind as well? By expanding your concept of ministry to include touching the lives of youth and adults in other Baptist churches, you are able to multiply the effectiveness of your ministry.

Experience opportunities for service and ministry.—As you become involved and influence the ministry of other churches, you are fulfilling opportunities for personal service and ministry. Local, state, and Convention events will afford you leadership experiences which may not be available within your own local church.

Participate in a network of support.—The Southern Baptist Convention was organized for the purpose of missions in 1845. Since then, each church in our Convention has acted as a free, independent, and autonomous body. We may best be referred to as a body with mutual dependency. We can do much more with others than we can by ourselves. All of us, both small and large churches, glean from the experiences of other churches. This unique support system of youth ministers from various sizes and types of churches provides fellowship, encouragement, evaluation, spiritual strength, and leadership development.

Become aware of denominational concerns.—Praying for our Convention becomes extremely difficult without a personal awareness of specific needs. By being involved with our denomination, we become better able to see realistically the problems and shortcomings as well as the rich heritage and promising vision of our Convention and know better how to pray for one another. This cannot be a concern left only for our pastors or a few select leaders. Youth ministers potentially are too strong a force of spiritual power to remain uninvolved and sit by idly.

Teach youth the role of our denomination.—We become models for our youth by the way we relate to and speak about our denomination. What we do or don't do is etched into the lives of our youth to pass on to the next generation. Every agency and board welcomes youth groups to visit their facilities and discuss their ministries. Firsthand experiences go a long way in teaching youth the ministries of our denomination.

Evaluating the Position

A recent letter to the editor in *The Baptist Record* was about a local minister of youth who was leaving the state for a new ministry. Having been a close friend of this minister of youth for many years, I read the letter with great interest.

The title the editor gave the letter was "A Young Man of Vision." A portion of this affirming letter, written by one of his peers, read:

> Not only has John had a model youth ministry . . . , but he has been a primary voice in visionary associational and state level youth ministry development in Mississippi. John has been co-chairman for the first two years for Mississippi Super Summer Youth Evangelism and Discipleship School. He has well represented the heartbeat for excellence that is beginning to shape and impact Mississippi Baptist Youth Ministry. . . . "Thank you for being a blessing, John, for always giving a 100 percent effort to our Lord, for crying with us, dreaming with us, and always attempting the impossible with us."[1]

How are you seen by your peers within your association, state, or Convention? Will you be recognized by others for crying, dreaming, and always attempting the impossible with them? Consider these broad positions for ministry available to you and ways to be involved with each right now.

Association

• Be willing to serve as the associational youth ministry coordinator.

The responsibilities of the youth ministry coordinator include:

1. Serves on the associational Pastoral Ministries council.

2. Enlists the support of church youth ministry coordinators (youth ministers, youth directors, etc.) for associational programs and events related to the youth program organizations.

3. Participates in planning associational projects which require the involvement of two or more youth program areas.

4. Provides an ongoing support group for church youth ministry coordinators.

5. Plans and promotes associational training and information conferences for church youth ministry coordinators.

6. Promotes state, regional, and national conferences for church ministry coordinators.

7. Reports progress of associational youth ministry coordinator work to the associational Pastoral Ministries director.[2]

• Sponsor associational events at your church.

• Take your youth to associational events (retreats, camps, rallies, etc.).

• Take your youth leaders to special training events.

• Use resources in your association such as BTN.

• Represent your church at the annual associational meeting.

• Organize or support a weekly or monthly support and fellowship meeting for ministers of youth.

State

• Volunteer for your state youth committee, if one exists. Write your state office for the name and responsibilities of your state consultant(s).

• Participate in state minister of youth conferences.

• Take youth to state events (evangelism conference, super summer, camps, retreats, training events, etc.).

• Take your youth leaders to special training events.

- Take your youth to your state office building.
- Represent your church at the annual state convention.

Convention

- Participate in regional or national conferences for ministers of youth.
- Support the church program organizations of our Convention. (This also can be done in your association and state.)
- Use denominational leadership resources in your church.
- Write for youth periodicals (ongoing curriculum, leadership, leisure reading).
- Take your youth to national youth events (Ridgecrest and Glorieta).
- Take youth to the denominational boards and agencies of our Convention (Sunday School Board and the Southern Baptist Convention Building in Nashville, Brotherhood Commission in Memphis, Woman's Missionary Union in Birmingham, Home Mission Board in Atlanta, Foreign Mission Board in Richmond, and the six Southern Baptist seminaries across the country).
- Take youth leaders to special national training events.
- Participate in the Baptist World Alliance.
- Represent your church at the annual Southern Baptist Convention.

Realm of Influence

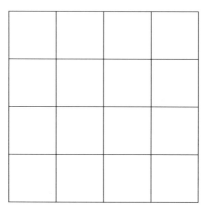

Quickly count the total number of squares in the diagram above.

Did you count 16? 17? 18? 22? 30? If your answer was the last number, you are correct! The problem here is that most of us limit ourselves to what we can see obviously. Count again. Do you see one whole square, 16 individual squares, 9 squares of 4 units each, and 4 squares of 9 units each?

Are you limiting your effectiveness in ministry? What is your realm of influence?

Are you aware of how many people you influence by your involvement with your association? You potentially can influence other local youth ministers, their youth, and their churches; your youth and your church; and yourself.

Are you aware of how many people you influence by your involvement with your state? You potentially can influence other associations in your state; youth ministers, their youth, and their churches in other associations in your state; your association; and all of those in your association.

Are you aware of how many people you influence by your involvement with your Convention? You potentially can influence our world, other states in our Convention, and many in your state and association.

By being involved only with your own local church, you limit your realm of influence with countless thousands of people.

Denominational Plan Sheet

Date _____

Ministry/Event	Contact Person (Name/Address/Phone #)
Purpose	Duties/Responsibilities Held
Notes (Use back if necessary.)	
Things to Do	
Evaluation	
Denominational Attitude Response	

Don't create the problem of limiting your effectiveness in ministry.

The Denominational Involvement Plan Sheet can be used with associational, state, and Convention ministries or events. It can serve as a useful tool as you participate in denominational events. Some ministries or events could include associational youth rallies, skating parties, retreats, camps, leadership training, etc.; state youth evangelism conferences, retreats, camps, leadership training, etc.; Convention national youth ministry conferences, Ridgecrest and Glorieta conferences, regional conferences, special workshops, etc.

Complete this plan sheet for every denominational ministry orevent. It can be useful not only in planning meetings but also as you and your church participate in such events.

Reproduce the Denominational Involvement Plan Sheet so that you can retain accurate records of your involvement in denominational events. File each under its ministry/event and refer to it when planning on attending future events.

Take a moment right now to copy the Denominational Involvement Plan Sheet. Think back to your last denominational ministry/event. Was it an associational, state, or Convention event?

Record the date of the event at the top of the plan sheet. Write the name of the event. Record the contact person, including his or her address and phone number.

Next, write down the purpose of the event. This should identify what the ministry or event was to accomplish. For example, if the event was an associational skating party, the purpose could read, "To provide an activity to have fun as well as to meet other Christian youth in our city." Also, "To present the gospel to lost youth by way of youth sharing personal testimonies after skating."

If you had any duties or responsibilities during this event, record these. This should include any leadership role.

The section entitled "Notes" is for you to record the control of the event. This could be an outline of a planning meeting or a summary of the event in which you participated.

In the section "Things To Do," record anything you needed to do after the event. For example, this might include making phone calls, writing thank-you letters or setting up a room.

Record your evaluation of the event. Honest and thorough evaluation will help you and others in planning future events.

In the "Denominational Attitude Response" section, reflect how this ministry/event has strengthened or supported your role in the denomination. Occasionally reread your comments in this section to see how your role in the denomination has changed, if any.

Now that you have had practice completing the Denominational Involvement Plan Sheet for a past event, you're ready for the next step. Look ahead on your calendar and identify the denominational ministries or events currently scheduled. Make a plan sheet for all events, and file them away until the time of the events.

"My Brother and I . . ."

The story of Will and Charlie parallels the potential youth ministers have by working with one another. These two brothers grew up at a time when surgery was still in its infancy.

Following in their father's footsteps as a doctor, Will graduated from the University of Michigan Medical School in 1883 and Charlie from the Chicago Medical School in 1888. One year later, their 70-year old father and both brothers became physicians at the St. Mary's Hospital in Rochester, Minnesota.

Will and Charlie were not only scientists but humanitarians as well. Even though more than one thousand scientific papers about their work were published in medical journals, their most famous marks came by the way they helped the less fortunate. As many as 30 percent of their patients never received a bill, and people were never charged more than 10 percent of their annual income. Also, every dollar received on bills which were over $1,000 was given to help other sick people.

For more than 70 years, Will and Charlie remained as close as two brothers could be. Charlie died unexpectedly of pneumonia on May 26, 1939; and Will, who was already ill, quietly died two months later.

Their success in life was seen not only as the famous founding surgeons of the Mayo Clinic, but Dr. Will Mayo and Dr. Charlie Mayo demonstrated a real success as brothers. Whenever either one received an honor, whether from the community, a university, or a government, each would begin his acceptance speech with the words, "My brother and I."

The story of the Mayo brothers provides all youth ministers with a potentially powerful thought. Like two brothers born to this world from the same parents, we, too, are born again through our faith and growing relationship with a caring Father. Though we may attend different schools in preparing for our ministries, we hold to the same purposes in meeting the needs of the youth to whom we minister. Even the caring and sharing spirits of the brothers parallel the servant spirit we demonstrate to others. Their support for one another should also not go unnoticed. For in many ways, the effectiveness of our own ministry depends largely on how we support those near us who are also seeking to accomplish our common goal.

As we support the whole we see that what one cannot do alone can now be done with others. As you minister in your church, association, state, and Convention, allow yourself to serve cooperatively with your fellow ministers of youth and rejoice with every opportunity to say, "My brother and I."

---

[1]Rich Malone, "Letters to the Editor," *The Baptist Record*, 8 September 1988, 6.

[2]D. G. McCoury, "Program of Associational Pastoral Ministries Manual" (Nashville: Church Administration Department, 1987), 9.

PERSONAL LEARNING ACTIVITIES

1. What reasons do you have if you have not been active in denominational activities?

2. What new potential can you see for working in associational, state, and denominational youth events?

3. What are the benefits of denominational involvement?

4. What opportunities do you have or can you find for service?

GROUP LEARNING ACTIVITIES

The Group Learning Activities provide suggestions for four 60-minute periods. The leader may use the Personal Learning Activities as well as the content of the chapters. The leader should read carefully the chapters and follow the suggestions given in preparing for each session. Encourage each participant also to read and study the chapters prior to the sessions.

SESSION 1

Chapter 1: The Minister of Youth's Heritage
Chapter 2: The Minister of Youth's Calling and Characteristics
Chapter 3: The Minister of Youth's Preparation and Education

Goal
To guide the class to feel admiration for the growing professionalism and significance of ministers of youth, to reaffirm their calling to that ministry, and to make specific plans for strengthening their preparation for that calling.

Preparation
1. Prepare a time line, using butcher paper at least six feet long. Provide felt-tip markers.
2. Cut from paper two life-size silhouettes.
3. Prepare sheets of paper or card stock designed to look similar to a school report card. Provide one column for listing "Subjects" and one for listing "Grades."
4. Provide a podium for the debate. Enlist someone with a digital watch to serve as timekeeper.
5. Prepare sheets of paper to look similar to a contract. Add a

fancy border and an attractive title, "Personal Contract." If available, add a gold seal or sticker.

Agenda

1. Play music from the 1950s as the group arrives.

2. Divide the group into subgroups. Assign each subgroup one or more pages from chapter 1 to review. Ask each subgroup to place on the time line significant events that impacted the development of youth ministry.

3. Label one of the full-size silhouettes as "Youth Director: 1955" and the other as "Minister of Youth: (current year)." Ask group members to write characteristics on the two silhouettes.

4. Ask group members to share their call into youth ministry. After sharing, ask members to stand somewhere in the room. Ask members whose calls are similar to stand near one another.

5. Distribute the blank report cards. Ask members to find and list characteristics of effective youth ministers in chapter 2. These should be listed in short form under "Subjects" on the report cards. Ask members to give themselves a letter grade beside each characteristic. Then ask them to place a star beside two key strengths they bring to youth ministry and to circle an area they wish to strengthen.

6. Ask group members who have attended college and seminary to report to the group how their ministries have been strengthened by these experiences.

7. Divide the group into two subgroups for a debate. Assign one group to be "affirmative" and one to be "negative." Allow subgroups time to choose speakers and prepare their cases. Decide on time limits for speeches. Debate the topic: Resolved, that students anticipating going on to seminary should not major in Bible or religion while in college.

8. Distribute the blank "contracts." Ask each member to scan the section on continuing education in chapter 3. Ask members to complete their contracts, promising to complete a significant continuing education project before a specified due date.

9. Close with a prayer of thanksgiving concerning group members' calling to youth ministry.

SESSION 2

Chapter 4: The Minister of Youth's Philosophy of Youth Ministry
Chapter 5: The Minister of Youth's Work with Youth

Goal
To guide members to update their philosophies of youth ministry and to identify strengths and areas of needed growth they experience in relation to teenagers.

Preparation
1. Enlist four members to portray photographic models. Prepare large name tags for each model saying, "Let Me Do It," "Big Event," "Pastor," and "Balanced." Use a desk, four chairs, and possibly some artificial plants to resemble the set of a late-night talk show.
2. Prepare a large sheet of butcher paper or newsprint to resemble a youth ministry newsletter. Add a large title and lines to show where columns will fall.
3. Prepare for each member 8½-by-11-inch sheets of paper labeled "My Youth Ministry Philosophy."
4. Prepare one wall to resemble a public-school hallway. Consider preparing large sheets of paper to represent school lockers or classroom doors. Secure a microphone.
5. Secure a dozen drink cups and napkins.

Agenda
1. Introduce the "late-night talk show" with you (the group leader) seated behind the desk as host. Interview each of the "models," asking questions about that model or approach to youth ministry. Interview the balanced "model" last, stressing the advantages of that approach to youth ministry.
2. Ask the entire group to contribute article headlines and opening paragraphs to the giant newsletter. Ask them to do this reflecting the "balanced" approach to youth ministry.
3. Distribute the sheets labeled "My Youth Ministry Philosophy." Ask members to reflect on their reading before class with

the group. Then ask them to write the basic elements of their own philosophy of youth ministry.

4. Ask five members to participate in a role play. One will portray an adult journalist with a microphone. The others will portray 12-, 14-, 16-, and 17-year-old young people respectively. The scene takes place in a school hallway. The journalist should ask general questions about interests, schedules, fears, families, etc., giving the "youth" an opportunity to portray how various ages of youth differ on such subjects.

5. Divide the group into subgroups of three members. Ask each subgroup to write a one-paragraph description of a fictional, troubled youth. As each subgroup reads their description aloud, the other subgroups should call out specific steps a youth minister should take to affirm that youth. Crisis intervention steps should also be discussed if appropriate.

6. Divide the group into two subgroups. The two subgroups should face each other from opposite sides of the room. The subgroups should take turns calling out to the other a typical youth ministry activity, relationship, project, or emphasis. Then the other subgroup has twenty seconds to call out a way that event could creatively be made supportive of youth evangelism. If the two subgroups are large, spokespersons should be selected. Award one point for each answer. Subgroups failing to respond in twenty seconds lose a point. The highest score wins.

7. Invite members to pray in pairs that God would guide them to affirm their strengths and strengthen their weaknesses in their direct ministries with teenagers.

SESSION 3

Chapter 6: The Minister of Youth's Work with Adult Leaders
Chapter 7: The Minister of Youth's Work with Parents

Goal
To guide members to choose specific actions that could strengthen their ministries with workers and parents of youth.

Preparation

1. Use paint and scissors to make a three-foot-square sheet of paper look old. Roll the edges to resemble a treasure map scroll.

2. Collect four wooden sawhorses or cardboard substitutes to represent roadblocks. Place one of the following signs on each roadblock. "I don't have time" "I'm afraid of teenagers." "I'm not trained to teach." "I'm not sharp enough."

3. Prepare for each member small sheets of paper that resemble the forms on which medical doctors write prescriptions.

4. Collect an assortment of supplies useful in creating visual images. Include such items as construction paper, yarn, felt-tip markers, scissors, glue, tape, paper and plastic kitchen goods, newspapers, and magazines.

5. Prepare for each member a paper clock face approximately eight inches in diameter. Draw the hour, minute, and second hands so they divide the clock into thirds. (For example, make the time 12:20:40.)

6. Provide a skirted, eight-foot table for the panel. Enlist four parents of youth to serve on the panel. Try to mix sexes and ages of the parents.

Agenda

1. Ask the group to recall material found in chapter 6 and to call out possible sources for new youth workers. Record their responses as "treasure locations" on the scroll.

2. If the size of the room permits, ask the group to move around the room together. As the group comes to a "roadblock," discuss ways to overcome that objection. Then walk together to the next "roadblock."

3. Distribute the prescription forms to members. Based on their prior reading, ask them to list two or three training "remedies" their workers need in order to function more effectively.

4. Divide the group into subgroups of four. Ask each subgroup to role-play silently a life situation experienced by youth workers to which youth ministers should personally respond (examples: birth of a child, death of a parent). After each subgroup presents its silent role play, ask the other groups to identify the situation and suggest ministry responses.

5. Ask members to reread the 10 principles of effective parent ministry in chapter 7. Assign each principle to an individual or subgroup. Ask members to use the visual arts supplies to create a graphic representation of the assigned principle. Call for demonstrations and explanations.

6. Remind members their weeks are already full. New time given to an expanded ministry with parents may mean giving up some activities. Distribute the clock faces. Ask members to write on the clock several time users they are willing to give up in order to give a third of time to ministry to and with parents.

7. Invite the panel of parents to dialogue on the topic, "Help and Support I Need from a Youth Minister." Allow group members to ask questions of the panel.

8. Divide the group into four subgroups. Ask each of the parents on the panel to lead a subgroup in prayer for stronger parent and youth relationships.

SESSION 4

Chapter 8: The Minister of Youth's Administrative and Planning Skills
Chapter 9: The Minister of Youth's Role with the Denomination

Goal
To guide members to value needs-based planning and to choose to avoid administrative weaknesses and hindrances to denominational support.

Preparation
1. Prepare two three-foot-square sheets of paper to resemble one-month youth calendars.

2. Tape five, five-foot sections of rope to the wall. Position the ropes so that each forms a complete circle similar to a cowboy's lariat. Tape eight four-by-six-inch cards to the wall in the same area but not inside any of the rope circles.

3. Secure four white plastic bleach bottles (one gallon size). Remove the paper labels and use a black marker to make the skull and crossbones poison symbol. Under the poison symbol, write one of the four administrative dangers in chapter 8.

4. Use black yarn and tape to form a large spider's web in the corner of the room. Use two walls and the ceiling. Add a large, plastic spider if available. On white pieces of paper write the sevenkey words found in chapter 9. Tape them in the spider's web.

Agenda

1. Divide the group into two subgroups. Ask each to write a brief description of some of the key strengths, problems, and weaknesses of a fictional youth ministry. When completed, ask the subgroups to exchange lists. Then ask the groups to fill in the giant calendars with programming directly related to the issues identified. Ask each subgroup to report its work.

2. Ask the group to call out eight youth activities or events that are often planned and conducted by a youth minister acting almost alone. Write these on the eight cards near the ropes. Ask the group to brainstorm ways each event could be channeled through one of the ongoing youth organizations. Label each of the lasso loops as one of the following: Youth Sunday School, Youth Discipleship Training, High School Baptist Young Men, Acteens, Pioneer Royal Ambassadors, and youth music. As the group captures a "stray" event for an organization, move the card containing that event to the appropriate lasso loop.

3. Ask several group members to demonstrate and explain the "to do" system they use each day to ensure all tasks are calendared and completed.

4. Place the four "poison" bottles in the four corners of the room. Ask each member to stand in the corner with the "poison" that represents the greatest temptation. Discuss each "poison." Ask the three groups not standing in a particular corner to describe ways they have found to manage that "poison."

5. Refer to the spider's web and the possible ways to get "caught" in a cycle of poor denominational support. Ask individual members who now support the denomination to share how they moved beyond the seven hindrances.

6. Provide time for reflection on the course of study, celebration for new or deeper relationships, and a closing time of meditation and commitment.